HIEVING EARLY YEARS
ROFESSIONAL STATUS

ACHIEVING EARLY YEARS PROFESSIONAL STATUS

DENISE REARDON

Los Angeles | London | New Delhi
Singapore | Washington DC

First published 2009

Reprinted 2010

SAGE Publications Ltd
1 Oliver's Yard
55 City Road
London EC1Y 1SP

SAGE Publications Inc.
2455 Teller Road
Thousand Oaks, California 91320

SAGE Publications India Pvt Ltd
B1/I1 Mohan Cooperative Industrial Area
Mathura Road
New Delhi 110 044

SAGE Publications Asia-Pacific Pvt Ltd
33 Pekin Street #02-01
Far East Square
Singapore 048763

Library of Congress Control Number: 2008937995

British Library Cataloguing in Publication data

A catalogue record for this book is available from the British Library

ISBN 978-1-84787-189-3
ISBN 978-1-84787-190-9 (pbk)

Typeset by C&M Digitals (P) Ltd, Chennai, India
Printed in Great Britain by TJ International, Padstow, Cornwall
Printed on paper from sustainable resources

Mixed Sources
Product group from well-managed
forests and other controlled sources
www.fsc.org   Cert no. SGS-COC-2482
© 1996 Forest Stewardship Council
FSC

For Ella Washington, an inspirational Mother, Grandmother, teacher, Early Years Advisor, EYP and EYP mentor whose work has influenced many young children and Early Years Professionals.

CONTENTS

ACKNOWLEDGEMENTS

A special thank you to Mike, Kirsten, Sarah, all my family and friends for all their love and support. Thank you to Jude Bowen, Amy Jarrold and the team at SAGE for believing in me. Thank you also to Vikki Bennet, Principal Lecturer at Bath Spa University, for her positive review of the book featured on Amazon. This book has been written in acknowledgment of the contribution made by so many of my past and present early years' colleagues, leaders and managers who taught me so much, especially Claire Alfrey, Christine Richie, Liz Hryniewicz, Angela Nurse, and Tony Booth at Canterbury Christ University, Dympna Reed at Advisory Services Kent, Terry Bolton, Terry Knight and Malcolm Bell at North West Kent FE College. Last but by no means least I wish to thank all the early years' leaders, managers and practitioners that I have been so privileged to work with in Kent and Medway Local Authorities. Over the years, in my various roles, I have been fortunate enough to engage in practice in their settings, exchange views at training sessions and participate in various partnership activities; I have learnt so much from you all. Without everyone's support, insightfulness, expertise, observations and discussions over the years this book would never have been written. I truly feel that everyone's contribution is reflected in what I have said in my first book about leading effective early years practice.

Finally, I would also like to thank the following people:

Tara Anwar and her team at Little Explorers Day Nursery, Borstal, Kent
Peter Michelle and his team at Mr. Noah's Pre-school, Iden Green, Kent
Alison Goodsell from Advisory Services Kent
Alison Walker and her team at St Peter's Nursery, Maidstone, Kent

for allowing me to take the photographs in their settings. Any omissions or mistakes are entirely my own.

ABOUT THE AUTHOR

Denise started out as a 'playschool helper mum', and later trained as an early years/primary school teacher specializing in creativity. She worked as a teacher in a number of primary schools across Kent and later at Canterbury FE College, training early years students and teaching assistants. She later took up the position of Head of Early Years at North West Kent (NWK) FE College. At NWK College, Denise held leadership responsibility for Health and Social Care as well as Early Years training, she led a large team of gifted and talented multi-disciplinary early years practitioners and health, social care programme leaders, lecturers and assessors. While at NWK College, Denise developed and ran CACHE, BTEC and City & Guilds Level 2 and 3 National Diploma, National Certificate and NVQ awards as well as HNDS and FD awards in partnership with Greenwich University, for early years teaching assistants and health and social care students. In addition she also held line management responsibility for the two 65 place nurseries.

While at NWK College, Denise enrolled on an international MBA and undertook a range of research and studies in Educational Management. As part of these studies Denise visited a number of French and Danish schools and pre-schools.

Her interest in leadership continued to be developed whilst working for Kent Local Authority where she was fortunate enough to work with a wide range of inspirational leaders from early years settings and work on projects inspired by Professor Ferre Laevers from the Leuven Institute in Belgium and Reggio Emilia Italy. In 2006 she became senior lecturer at Canterbury Christ Church University where she teaches on the BA (hons) and Foundation Degree Early Years programmes. She became the EYPS Programme Director in January 2007, during the second phase of the project and leads the EYPS programme being run in partnership with the University of Chichester (UoC) with her colleague Ruth Bradley, the EYPS Programme Coordinator at UoC. Her passion for leadership and team work and her continuing interest in the early years sector has encouraged her to write this book, which draws together nearly 30 years of her experience of working alongside students and colleagues passionate about providing excellent services for children.

KEY TO ICONS

The following is a key to the icons used:

Chapter Objectives

Leadership Activity

Case Study

Written Activity

Points for Reflection

Key Points

Points to Remember

Further Reading

Reflective Activity

Useful Websites

PREFACE: HOW TO USE THIS BOOK

The future of the Early Years looks very promising indeed. With the government's vision to professionalize the childcare workforce (*Children's Workforce Strategy*, DfES, 2006a), raising the qualification level of the early years workforce sits at the heart of transforming the sector.

The purpose of this book is to support early years colleagues, graduates and those undertaking Early Years Professional Status (EYPS), in their understanding and reflection of the Children's Workforce Development Council (CWDC), the EYPS validation and assessment process and the associated 39 National Standards. The book is based on my own personal experience and supported throughout by reference to early years literature, research evidence and government policies and initiatives. The philosophy behind this book is that in order to achieve the Government's Workforce Strategy aim to develop a world-class workforce and improve outcomes for children, practitioners and graduates must be afforded equal guidance and support to become reflective practitioners in their training and development.

There is a clear need for a book to examine and critique government policy, frameworks and guidance and relevant research and theory to support early years leaders to gain Early Years Professional Status (EYPS). With the government's childcare strategy aiming to establish 3500 Sure Start Children's Centres by 2010, with an EYP in each setting, and one in every full-daycare setting by 2015, the emphasis on the Early Years Professional (EYP) to radicalize early years provision is tremendous.

This book was written to meet that need, and is designed to support the training and development of both existing early years practitioners and graduates who are new to the sector. It can be used by practitioners and graduates accessing any of the EYPS pathways set by the Children's Workforce Development Council (CWDC). The extent to which EYPS pathway you will be following will very much depend upon the level of early years qualification and experience that you have in working with babies, toddlers and young children. Below is an outline of the pathways:

- **The four-month part-time validation only**: for practitioners who meet the entry requirements and who are very experienced in working with babies, toddlers and young children and are close to meeting the EYPS standard.
- **The six-month, short, part-time extended professional development**: for practitioners that are not experienced in working with all the age ranges in 0–5 years. They may be more experienced with one age range than another and need to gain additional knowledge, skills and understanding.
- **The fifteen-month, long, part-time extended professional development**: for practitioners that have a level 5 qualification such as an Early Years Foundation degree or those that require longer placements or training to develop their knowledge, skills and understanding. Practitioners with a level 5 qualification will be able to top up to a full degree.
- **The full training pathway**: lasting 12 months full time, for non-early-years-related graduates who have little or no experience of working with children in the age range of 0–5 years.
- The CWDC are also developing new routes.

The book supports the reader's understanding that whichever pathway is followed, he or she must have a thorough knowledge and understanding of EYP's 39 standards by the time the final stage of the EYPS validation/assessment process is undertake. The book invites the reader to reflect on the CWDC, EYPS standards which are organized under the following six areas:

- knowledge and understanding
- effective practice
- relationships with children
- communicating and working in partnership with families and carers
- team work and collaboration
- professional development.

The chapters in this book are organized in such a way so as to lead the reader on a reflective journey.

Chapter 1: Getting Started provides an introduction to Early Years Professional Status. This chapter will set the scene for the EYPS, what it is and why it is so important to give credibility to the early years sector. It will examine the changes outlined in *Every Child Matters: Change for Children* within the context of providing the EYPS for the early years sector. By examining the early years sector's history and background, it will help to contextualize where the transformational early years practitioners' role might be heading in the future.

Chapter 2: What Is the EYPS Process? This chapter provides an introduction to the format of the validation process which is the same for each pathway. It is necessary to consider this at the beginning of the book, as practitioners will need to demonstrate that they meet the characteristics outlined in each of the standards for the EYPS by the time they are ready for final validation.

Chapter 3: What Qualities, Knowledge, Skills and Understanding Does an EYP Need to Have? This chapter will explore the knowledge and understanding that is identified in the EYPS standard and ways in which it can underpin a practitioner's ability to lead, model and establish ways to put the standards into practice.

Chapter 4: What Is Effective Practice? This chapter will explore the holistic nature of effective practice within the context of developing the practitioner's ability to lead, model, plan and provide safe and appropriate child-led and adult-initiated experiences, activities and play opportunities both indoors and outdoors for babies, young children and toddlers. It will also consider how to lead and promote ways of giving sensitive feedback to help children aged 0–5 years understand what they have achieved and think about what they need to do next and, when appropriate, encourage children aged 0–5 years to think about, evaluate and improve their own performance.

Chapter 5: Early Years Effective Practice – Assessment Arrangements, Routines and Communication, Language and Literacy will explore ways that the EYP can lead, model and establish fair, respectful, trusting, supportive and constructive relationships with children. The chapter will also consider how the EYP leads and supports other early years professionals to communicate sensitively and effectively with children aged 0–5 years and maintain effective assessment arrangements and routines that support individual children's needs.

Chapter 6: Protecting Effective Practice will explore ways that the EYP can lead, model and establish effective health and safety measures, and ways of safeguarding children, and make provision for the Early Years Foundation Stage (2008) welfare requirements.

Chapter 7: Relationships with Children, Families and Carers will explore ways that the EYP can lead, model and establish ways to recognize and respect the influences and contribution that parents and carers can make to children's development, well-being and learning. It will also look at ways to provide formal and informal opportunities through which information about children's well-being, development and learning can be shared between the parents and the setting.

Chapter 8: Sustaining Team Work and Collaboration and Professional Development Needs will explore how the EYP can lead, model and establish ways to build a team culture of collaborative and cooperative working between colleagues in early years settings. It will examine ways in which the EYP can promote an understanding to colleagues about their individual roles and responsibilities and the contribution that they make towards helping babies, young children and toddlers meet planned objectives.

Chapter 9: Going through the Gateway, Chapter 10: Beyond the Gateway and **Chapter 11: The Final Stages of the EYPS Validation Process – The Setting Visit** will be given to exploring ways in which practitioners aiming to gain the EYPS can demonstrate their leadership and a support of others and their own practice required for the validation and assessment of the Gateway Review, Written Tasks and the Setting Visit process. The book offers a practical insight into the way that the 39 EYPS standards are organized. The reflective tasks set out in each chapter will help you to determine the ways that you can demonstrate in your own practice the knowledge, skills and understanding that will be required of each standard by the time you reach the final stages of the EYPS validation and assessment process. More importantly, you will be encouraged to unpick the content within each standard to reflect on how it underpins your practice and informs your leadership and support of others.

During my exciting working career in leading, managing, training and mentoring a wide range of early years professionals, practitioners often spoke to me about working in the Cinderella sector. They often talked about being undervalued and not being recognized for all the hard work and effort that they put in. I believe that EYPS now provides the opportunity to gain that recognition. It is easy to identify that the one thing that keeps us all in the early years sector is our passion for children and wanting to make a difference. At a time when we are facing an unprecedented change and the transformation of the early years sector, it is vital that those working within it are equipped professionally to meet the new challenges. This book will encourage you to engage in self-reflection about your personal leadership role, your decision-making abilities and the ways that you communicate change and promote effective practice to others. The book will examine research related to the notion that outcomes for children and families are much better supported when practitioners are well qualified and possess a good understanding about child development and learning.

CHAPTER 1

GETTING STARTED – AN INTRODUCTION TO EARLY YEARS PROFESSIONAL STATUS

This chapter sets the scene for the Early Years Professional Status (EYPS), what it is and why it is so important to give credibility to the early years sector. It will examine the changes outlined in *Every Child Matters: Change for Children* (DfES, 2003b) within the context of providing the EYPS for the early years sector. This chapter will examine the changes implemented by the government to professionalize the early years workforce in England. It will look at the government's strategy and the way that it has influenced a response to develop the role of the Early Years Professional (EYP).

This chapter will also identify certain key research findings that have influenced the sector-wide changes and the government vision to develop a world-class workforce that will lead to better outcomes for children, parents, carers and society. By examining an overview of the national policies introduced this millennium, it will help to contextualize where the transformational Early Years Professional role might be heading in the future.

Background to the Early Years Workforce Reforms

Early education and care has received considerable attention this millennium and the Labour Government in England has pledged the availability for parents of more childcare places, better quality early education and care, and greater choice and accessibility. In 2006, the first ever legislation specific to early childhood education and care received royal assent. The Childcare Act 2006 places a statutory duty on Local Authorities to take lead responsibility for childcare in partnership with others to raise quality, improve delivery and achieve better results. A further priority is to develop more integrated provision that seeks to improve well-being and reduced inequalities in relation to the five outcomes of *Every Child Matters* (DfES, 2003b).

Every Child Matters sets out five outcomes that matter most to children and young people:

- **Being healthy**: enjoying good physical and mental health and living a healthy lifestyle.
- **Staying safe**: being protected from harm and neglect.
- **Enjoying and achieving**: getting the most out of life and developing the skills for adulthood.
- **Making a positive contribution**: being involved with the community and not engaging in anti-social or offending behaviour.
- **Economic well-being**: not being prevented by economic disadvantage from achieving full potential in life.

The government's aspiration to change the early years workforce is outlined in the *Children's Plan: Building Brighter Futures* (DCSF, 2007b) and *Every Child Matters: Change for Children* (DfES, 2003b) and provides the context for the government reforms. Running parallel to this is a number of early years research initiatives to include the DfES-funded longitudinal study of Effective Provision of Pre-school Education (EPPE; Sylva et al., 2004) which has influenced the government's commitment to provide high-quality, pre-school childcare provision for children, parents, carers and society in general as recognized in the government's *Ten-year Childcare Strategy: Choice for Parents – The Best Start for Children* (DfES, 2004a). The strategy not only champions the development of high-quality childcare provision but also signals the notion that working with pre-school children should have as much status as a profession as teaching children in schools. The strategy proposes a review of the qualifications and career structures of the early years workforce as well as a significant investment in training and support.

The government undertook a consultation with early years stakeholders about the proposals outlined in the children's workforce strategy through the *Children's Workforce Strategy: A Strategy to Build a World-class Workforce for Children and Young People – Consultation Document* (2005a). The consultation revealed that there was widespread support for the new role of Early Years Professional (EYP) to be introduced to those practitioners leading early years practice in the early years sector. Following the *Children's Workforce Strategy: The Government's Response to the Consultation* (DfES, 2006a), the government set out its aspiration to develop a first-class workforce and a commitment to develop the EYP role. It should be acknowledged that in order to achieve the government's vision to transform the early years sector in light of the vision for the new EYP role, it will rely on early years practitioners being much more accountable for the delivery of high-quality childcare and education and the achievement of better outcomes for children and their families as the EPPE report (Sylva et al., 2004) research evidence suggests.

The key challenges that are relevant to the new EYP role were presented in the *Children's Workforce Strategy: The Government's Response to the Consultation* (DfES, 2006a). They include:

- recruiting more people into working in the early years workforce
- developing and training existing practitioners in the early years workforce
- strengthening ways of integrated working and developing new workforce roles across the early years workforce
- improving and strengthening leadership and management roles in the early years workforce.

While the government's proposal to address these key challenges is outlined in *Choice for Parents, the Best Start for Children: A Ten-year Strategy for Childcare* (DfES, 2004a), one of the biggest ramifications for early years practitioners with existing leadership and management roles and for those of you who aspire to become future leaders and managers is that you will be required to gain higher academic qualifications. For many early years managers and leaders, this will mean accessing an Early Years Foundation degree (FD) or Bachelor of Arts (BA) degree at a local university. *Choice for Parents, the Best Start for Children* (DfES, 2004a) calls for:

- leaders with higher qualifications
- trained teachers working alongside and supporting other staff
- practitioners having a good understanding of child development and learning.

The action plan *acknowledges that at the time of publication*, the number of graduate-level leaders in early years settings, outside schools, was very low, particularly in the private and voluntary and independent (PVI) sectors. Traditionally, it was the requirement for early years leaders and managers to be qualified up to level 3, many of whom would have gained a National Diploma or a NVQ from awarding bodies such as CACHE (Council for Awards in Children's Education) or BTEC Edexcell. The Children's Workforce Strategy recommends that the following roles can be linked to qualification levels:

- Level 2 – assistant early years practitioner
- Level 3 – early years practitioner
- Level 4 – senior early years practitioner
- Level 5 – assistant early years professional
- Level 6 – early years professional at an equivalent level to qualified teachers
- Level 7 – leader/manager.

As part of the government's aspiration to raise the skills and the academic qualification levels amongst the early years workforce, it was announced that the Children's Workforce Development Council (CWDC) would take the lead on any development work and on the investment to support the training and development of early years professionals. Working closely with the government and its partners, the CWDC determined the qualification levels for early years leaders and the direction of workforce reforms. CWDC introduced the first phase of EYPS training pathways for early years professionals at graduate level (level 6) in 2006. To achieve EYPS, practitioners will need to demonstrate that they meet CWDC (2006), 39 National Standards working with babies, toddlers and young children to the end of the Early Years Foundation Stage (EYFS). The standards for EYPS support the Every Child Matters agenda (2004), the ten-year childcare strategy *Choice for Parents, the Best Start for Children* (DfES, 2004a); the Childcare Act 2006; and the introduction of the EYFS (2008). Combined, these strategies reflect the government and CWDC's vision that over time practitioners holding EYPS will become early years workforce 'change agents' and will use their high-level professional skills and abilities to transform the early years sector, thus providing better outcomes for all children by:

- raising the quality of early years provision
- leading practice across the EYFS
- supporting and mentoring other practitioners
- modelling the skills and behaviours that safeguard and support children.

While recognizing the diversity of the early years workforce, CWDC (2006) also believes that practitioners with EYPS should be leading practice in all children's centres offering childcare by 2010, and in every full-daycare setting by 2015.

Funding the Early Years Workforce Reforms

The Transformation Fund 2006 set out to support Local Authorities in the training and development of early years practitioners, and the appointment of graduate-status practitioners, mainly in the private, voluntary and independent sectors, where levels of qualifications are deemed to be lower than those in the maintained sector.

The CWDC investment formed part of the Transformation Fund 2006 of £250m over two years, which was announced alongside the response to the Workforce Strategy consultation (DfES, 2006a). The Transformation Fund 2006 was introduced initially as a two-year initiative to test out approaches to workforce development in the early years sector, and included:

- training to achieve Early Years Professional Status
- a recruitment incentive for full-daycare settings with newly employed staff with relevant graduate qualifications
- a quality premium for full-daycare settings that already employ or recruit at least one employee with relevant graduate-level qualifications
- training to levels 3 to 5.

The CWDC allocated £52m from the Transformation Fund (TF) to cover the costs for: developing and delivering appropriate training routes to EYP status, both for those currently working in the sector and those wishing to join it in the future, and, the costs of fees, bursaries, supply cover and mentoring for those working full day and for staff in full-daycare settings and Sure Start Children's Centres who wish to reach EYP status. The TF was superceded by the Graduate Leader Fund (GLF)

Table 1.1   *Key early years reforms Timeline*

Date	Milestone event
February 2006	Local authorities received Transformation Fund allocation letters
March 2006	Transformation Fund Guidance issued
April 2006	Implementation Plan for the Ten Year Strategy for Childcare
April 2006	Transformation Fund available for level 3–5 training and training to support children with additional needs
April 2006	General Sure Start Grant: Memorandum of Grant 2006–07
April – June 2006	Consultation on EYPS Standards informing the Prospectus. HEIs (and other providers) plan for delivery of EYPS
June 2006	EYP Prospectus with agreed standards, training routes etc.
September 2006	Transformation Fund available for Quality Premiums, Recruitment Incentives and Home Grown Graduate Incentives
From September 2006	Pilot training for those close to EYPS on the 3 month validation path
September 2006	LA and Providers providing first of 6 monthly returns on Transformation Fund performance
December 2006	07–08 Transformation Fund allocations confirmed
December 2006	Changes and clarifications were made to the Transformation Fund conditions covered in this Guidance, the confirmation of allocations letter to local authorities on 15 December and the updated Frequently Asked Questions
January 2007	First EYPS Status accreditation conferred
From January 2007	Training for EYPS available more widely through HEIs and other training providers
March/April 2007	LA and Providers provide second of 6 monthly returns on Transformation Fund performance
Summer/Autumn 2007	CSR 2007 announcement which will determine Transformation Fund beyond August 2008. [Superseding Graduate Leader Fund announced]
2007	First biennial review of the Transformation Fund
2008	A higher proportion of the early years workforce in all settings qualified to at least level 3 by 2008
August 2008	2006–08 initial Transformation Fund allocation ends. Future funding to be determined within the CSR 2007 [Graduate Leader Fund introduced April 2008 with 'in principle' funding support from the Government through to 2015]
2010	Every Children's Centre offering early years provision has an EYP
2015	Every full daycare setting has an EYP

Source: Transformation Fund Guidance (Revised 2007)

Points for Reflection

Look at EYPS standard S38

- ✓ Reflect on the impact that the government reforms in Table 1.1 have made on your professional role and those of your team
- ✓ What decisions have you made about your own or your staff's professional development needs as a result of the government reforms?
- ✓ Why are you aspiring to become an EYP?
- ✓ Have you accessed the GLF and how are you planning to use it?

Point to Remember

'Leadership is linked to learning, early childhood practitioners will learn from one another because the leader subtly nurtures collaborative learning by acting as a model, learner and facilitator.' (Solly in Rodd, 2006: 7)

Reforming the Early Years Workforce

The government's policy and aspiration to create a highly skilled workforce for the early years sector is based on research evidence – for example, amongst other studies, the DfES-funded longitudinal study of Effective Provision of Pre-school Education (EPPE; Sylva et al., 2004). The study highlights the importance of providing good quality stable early education and care experiences for early childhood social, behavioural, emotional, psychological, physical and cognitive development and their well-being now and in their futures'. Key EPPE findings suggest that the higher the staff qualifications, the more developmental progress children make in the pre-school period.

The *Key Elements of Effective Practice* (KEEP; DfES, 2005b) is informed by the EPPE study (Sylva et al., 2004) and is significant for EYP's leading practice as it supports the belief that in order for children to achieve better outcomes, they need to be afforded childcare provision that fosters secure relationships and offers an appropriate learning environment with high-quality teaching and learning experiences.

KEEP – The Key Elements of Effective Practice

Effective practice in the early years requires committed, enthusiastic and reflective practitioners with a breadth and depth of knowledge, skills and understanding. Effective practitioners use their own learning to improve their work with young children and their families in ways which are sensitive, positive and non-judgemental. Therefore, through initial and ongoing training and development, practitioners need to develop, demonstrate and continuously improve their:

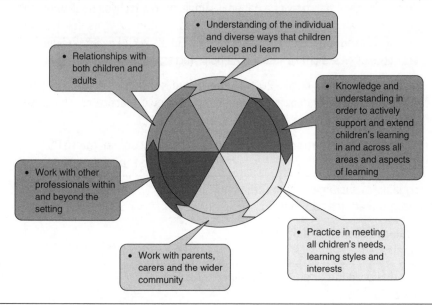

- Understanding of the individual and diverse ways that children develop and learn
- Relationships with both children and adults
- Knowledge and understanding in order to actively support and extend children's learning in and across all areas and aspects of learning
- Work with other professionals within and beyond the setting
- Practice in meeting all chidren's needs, learning styles and interests
- Work with parents, carers and the wider community

Figure 1.1   *KEEP: The Key Elements of Effective Practice* (DfES, 2005)

To become an EYP, you can use the KEEP (DfES, 2005b) framework as an evaluation tool as it offers an outline of the areas of knowledge, skills and understanding required to promote effective early years practice. Areas of effective practice offered by KEEP include the importance of working in partnerships with parents, carers and the wider community, as well as working with a range of multi-disciplinary professionals to deliver an integrated approach to services for young children and their families which is also at the heart of the *Every Child Matters* (DfES, 2003b) Sure Start agenda.

Early Years Regulation and Inspection

As an EYP, you will be expected to have a sound working knowledge of the national and local statutory and non-statutory frameworks that you work within, and at the same time adopt a suitable leadership style that will empower your early years colleagues to bring about change and implement the policies and practice within your early years setting.

✝✝✝✝   Leadership Activity

The Effective Provision of Pre-School Education (EPPE; Sylva et al., 2004) project is the first major European longitudinal study of a national sample of young children's development (intellectual and social/behavioural) between the ages of 3 and 7 years. The following website will provide you with a copy of the EPPE (Sylva et al., 2004) report on Sure Start: www.surestart.gov.uk/research/keyresearch/ eppe/ (accessed on 12 April 2008).

Read the EPPE (Sylva et al., 2004) report, and consider the ways in which your knowledge and understanding underpin your own practice and leadership of others against the areas listed below:

EPPE (2004) recommendations for working with 3–5 year-olds:	Look at the EYPS standards:
✓ The quality of sustained shared thinking between the adult and the child	⇒ S16
✓ The balance between adult-led and child-initiated activities	⇒ S11
✓ A strong knowledge and understanding of the EYFS	⇒ S1
✓ Knowledge of child development and how children learn	⇒ S2
✓ Development of colleagues' skills and qualification levels	⇒ S38
✓ Encouragement of high levels of parental engagement with their children's learning	⇒ S1, S29, S30, S31, S32
✓ Encouragement of behaviour policies where colleagues support behaviour management through reasoning and talk	⇒ S17, S35

Point to Remember

'Empowerment is what leaders give to their people; self-leadership is what people do to make empowerment work.' (Blanchard, 2007: 107)

✝✝✝✝   **Leadership Activity**

Review KEEP (DfES, 2005b)

The following website will provide you with a copy of KEEP:

www.standards.dfes.gov.uk/primary/publications/foundation_stage/keep/

What knowledge and understanding do you have for each of the key elements of effective practice in Figure 1.1?

How do you use this knowledge and understanding to inform your personal practice and leadership and support of others:

Key Elements of Effective Practice:	Look at the EYPS Standards:
✓ Promoting an understanding of the individual and diverse ways that children learn?	⇒ S2
✓ The supporting and extending of children's learning across all the areas of the EYFS?	⇒ S1, S3, S6, S11, S14
✓ Meeting children's needs, learning styles and interests?	⇒ S2, S3, S7, S8, S9
✓ Working with parents and carers and the wider community?	⇒ S29, S30, S31, S32
✓ Working with other professionals within and beyond your setting?	⇒ S6, S33, S36
✓ Developing strong relationships with children and adults?	⇒ S25, S26, S27

The Childcare Act 2006 included provisions to reform the regulation and inspection regime for childcare in England, meeting a commitment set out in the government's ten-year strategy for childcare, *Choice for Parents: The Best Start for Children* (DfES, 2004a). The provisions include the establishment of an early years register for childcare for children up to the age of five and a register for childcare for children aged five and over (the Ofsted Childcare Register). Information specific to childcare that is suitable for disabled children states that all provision must comply with the Disability Discrimination Act 2005. Information for providers and parents about the government's family-focused services for young disabled children and their families across England is found in the government's Early Support programme (DCSF, 2007b). The programme was developed as part of the restructuring of children's services in response to the government green paper, *Every Child Matters*, and alongside the new integrated assessment, information and inspection frameworks for children's services. The programme is funded by the Department for Children, Schools and Families (DCSF) through the Sure Start Unit and has been developed in conjunction with the Department of Health and the voluntary sector.

While the programme has been developed specifically for children under the age of three, the DCSF has suggested that the principles underlying Early Support are applicable to all children under five.

 Point for Reflection

One objective of the Childcare Act 2006 is to highlight the importance of involving parents in the design and delivery of services to ensure that they best meet local needs.

Consider the ways in which you involve parents in the care and education of all children.

Look at the EYPS standards:

⇒ S29, S30, S31, S32

 Point to Remember

'Key issues for research continue to be how to involve parents in ways which are inclusive, participative, respectful and meaningful. Some settings have developed an international reputation for their work in involving parents in their children's learning, for example the Pen Green Centre (Arnold, 2001; Whalley et al., 1997), the Coram Children's Centre in London (Draper and Duffy, 2001) and the Sheffield Children's Centre.' (Nutbrown, 2006: 98)

The Childcare Act 2006 also introduced a new, statutory curriculum for the early years (the Early Years Foundation Stage, from September 2008) for children from birth to five. Delivery was made compulsory from September 2008 for all registered early years providers, and a new (Ofsted) inspection framework introduced simultaneously.

It is envisaged that EYPs will be one of the key transformational leaders in the implementation of the Early Years Foundation Stage (EYFS) framework (DCSF, 2008b) which sets the standards for the learning, development and care of children from birth to five. The new framework extends and encompasses the statutory *Curriculum Guidance for the Foundation Stage* (DfEE, 2000), the non-statutory *Birth to Three Matters* framework (DfES, 2002), and the regulatory frameworks in the *National Standards for Under-8s Daycare and Childminding* (DfES, 2003a, with revisions in 2005).

The Early Years Foundation Stage (EYFS – see DCSF, 2008b) brings together learning, development and care of all children from birth to five. The EYFS will build on and replace the *Curriculum Guidance for the Foundation Stage* (DfEE, 2000), the *Birth to Three Matters* (DfES, 2002) framework and the *National Standards for Under-8s Daycare and Childminding* (DfES, 2003a), building a coherent and flexible approach to care and learning. EYPS are required to lead on the requirements set out in the EYFS. Parents can be sure that there will be the same standards of learning and care for their children irrespective of the setting they attend.

This duty supports EYPs since it places a responsibility on Local Authority officers to know what childcare is available, when and where in different parts of the country. This information will help EYPs to assess what type of provision, if any, they should consider providing for parents and carers and the potential market for uptake of childcare places by people in their vicinity. In addition, the localisation of childcare responsibility has brought about devolved funding, bringing opportunities defined in the Care Standards Act 2000 which sets out legally who needs to register with Ofsted as a daycare provider. This was supported and enacted through a set of National Standards that all such providers must meet (as was mentioned earlier, these vary according to the type of care that is provided). Changes to the registration regulations have come about as a result of the Childcare Act 2006, the precise details of which were published following a public consultation during February 2008. These changes are linked to the implementation of the new Early Years Foundation Stage (2008). Childminders responsible for the care of children up to eight years of age are also required to join the compulsory part of the Childcare Register.

The Childcare Act 2006 introduced two new registers, which are being operated by Ofsted: the Early Years Register (EYR) and the Ofsted Childcare Register (OCR) (2008). Childcare providers caring for children aged up to five are required to join the Early Years Register, unless exempt. The OCR has two parts:

EYPs who are childminders or childcare providers registered on the Early Years Register must be aware of the legal requirements set out in the Childcare Act 2006 and the associated regulations that must be met in order for their setting to remain registered.

The legal requirements set out in the *Statutory Framework for the Early Years Foundation Stage* (2007) specify the welfare, learning and development of young children as part of the Early Years Foundation Stage (EYFS) framework for children aged from birth up until the 31 August after their fifth birthday.

Providers must inform Ofsted (2008) about:

- Any change in the name or address of the childminder or the childcare provider.
- Any change in the name, registered number or registered address of a company or charity providing childcare.
- Any change to the address of the premises where the childcare is provided.
- The details of any changes to the premises where the childcare takes place. This includes changes that affect the space available or the quality of care available. One example is building work to extend or change premises.
- Any intention to change the hours that you provide childcare where such a change involves overnight care.
- The details of any allegations of serious harm to or abuse of a child by any person living, working or caring for children at the premises where the care is provided. The allegations of serious harm or abuse may have occurred on the premises or elsewhere. You must also tell us about any other alleged abuse that might have happened on the childcare premises. Whenever you give us this information you also need to tell us about the action you have taken.
- The details of any serious accident, serious illness, injury to, or death of, any child in your care and the action you have taken in response. As a general rule serious accidents and injuries are those requiring treatment by a medical practitioner. Serious illnesses, such as meningitis, are normally notifiable diseases: they are not the usual childhood illnesses such as chicken pox.
- Details of any incident of food poisoning where two or more children cared for on the premises are affected.
- Details of any other significant event that is likely to affect the suitability of the provider or any person who cares for, or is in regular contact with, children on the premises. For example, this could be a change in circumstances affecting a provider's physical or mental ability to care for children.
- Any change to the manager of the childcare provision – not for childminders.
- Any change of people aged 16-years or older living or working on the premises where the care is provided, including where children attain their sixteenth birthday. Working on the premises means that their work is done in the part of the premises where the care takes place and during the times when care takes place – childcare providers on domestic premises and childminders only.

Ofsted registration process looks at three main areas:

- the suitability of the person providing the care
- the suitability of other people associated with the registration such as the manager of a nursery or those who live with a childminder
- the suitability of the premises and equipment to make sure they are safe for childcare'.

Ofsted Inspections

Early Years Professionals leading provision that is registered on the EYR will be inspected during and after registration and then once every three years. Ofsted will regulate the provision to ensure the EYR and EYFS requirements are met, and will produce an inspections report.

The inspections are conducted under a common early years' evaluation schedule which is common to all Ofsted inspection frameworks. This is to ensure that early years provision in both schools and PVI early years settings is evaluated in the same way. The schedule includes key judgments that inspectors will make and what they will take into account when evaluating all types of early years provision.

Key judgments will be made across four areas:

- the effectiveness of provision in meeting the needs of children in the Early Years Foundation Stage
- how effectively the Years Foundation Stage is led and managed
- how effectively the children in the Early Years Foundation Stage are helped to learn and develop
- how effectively the welfare of the children in the Early Years Foundation Stage is promoted.

Inspectors evaluating and reporting on the leadership and management of the early years provision will take into account all the requirements of the EYFS including:

- the steps taken to promote improvement
- how well the setting works in partnership with parents and others
- how well children are safeguarded.

The central question for Early Years Professionals contributing to leading the overall effectiveness of the provision will be determined by the way that your own practice and your leadership of others ensures that the five Every Child Matters (ECM) outcomes meet the needs of all children who attend the setting. You will need to take into account the following aspects:

- how you routinely lead practice to meet the needs of all children
- how your own practice, leadership and support in the setting supports every child so that no group or individual is disadvantaged
- how your own practice, leadership and support encourages all children to make progress in their learning and development
- how you practice, lead and support others to ensure that children's welfare is promoted
- how you contribute to partnerships in the wider context to promote good quality education and care
- how your own practice, leadership and support contributes to effective planning for improvement, including the process of self evaluation.

Ofsted will grade the quality of provision using the scale of outstanding, good, satisfactory and inadequate.

Reflective Activity

1. What is your knowledge about the the main provisions of the national and local statutory and non-statutory frameworks related to the well-being, care and education of babies, toddlers and young children?
2. How do you lead and support colleagues in developing their understanding of statutory and non-statutory frameworks?

Examples of relevant national and local documents include:

✓ the policies and procedures of the Local Authority Safeguarding Children's Board
✓ local arrangements for identifing and supporting children with additional needs
✓ the *Statutory Framework for the Early Years Foundation Stage* (DCSF, 2008b)
✓ *Practice Guidance for the Early Years Foundation Stage* (DCSF, 2008a)
✓ *Every Child Matters* (DfES, 2003b)
✓ the Children Act 2004
✓ the *Code of Practice on the provision of free nursery education places* (DfES guidance) (DfES, 2006a)
✓ the Childcare Act 2006
✓ the Common Assessment Framework (CAF) (CWDC, 2006)
✓ the Early Support Programme for supporting SEN/disabled children
✓ Choice for Parents – The Best Start for Children – A Ten-year *Strategy for Childcare* (DfES, 2004a)
✓ the *Children's Plan: Building Brighter Futures* (DCSF, 2007b).

Look at the EYPS standards:

⇒ S1, S5, S35

Meeting Ofsted Learning and Development Requirements

The underpinning philosophies, values and belief systems that EYPs have developed through their graduate studies and their own practice will inform their leadership of others and their ability to model and provide appropriate play opportunities that will enable babies, toddlers and young children to make progress towards the early learning goals. Ofsted's central question is 'What is it like for a child here?'. EYPs can answer this question by reflecting on their own practice and their leadership and support of others in their setting, network or service to examine how:

- the needs of all children are routinely met
- every child receives support
- children make progress in their learning and development
- children's welfare is promoted
- partnerships in the wider context are used to promote good quality education and care
- planning for improvement, including the process of self evaluation is used effectively
- well the learning environment helps children progress towards the early learning goals
- the extent to which there is planned, purposeful play and exploration, both in and out of doors, with a balance of adult-led and child-led activities, results in children being active learners, creative and critical thinkers
- the quality of planning for individuals ensures that each child receives an enjoyable and challenging experience across the areas of learning
- information from observation and assessment is used to ensure that children achieve as much as they can in relation to their starting points and capabilities
- additional learning and/or development needs are identified and provided for.

---

††††   Leadership Activity

How do you lead and support others to deliver the Ofsted learning and development requirements?

These are concerned with providing appropriate opportunities to enable children to make progress towards the early learning goals – they are divided into six interrelated categories:

- ✓ Personal, social and emotional development
- ✓ Communication, language and literacy
- ✓ Problem solving, reasoning and numeracy
- ✓ Knowledge and understanding of the world
- ✓ Physical development
- ✓ Creative development
  (DCSF, 2008b:12–15)

Look at the EYPS standards:

- ⇒ S6, S19 – children's physical and emotional well-being
- ⇒ S10, S21 – using child observations
- ⇒ S15, S16, S22, S26, S27 – communication, language and literacy
- ⇒ S35 – planning child-led/adult-initiated activities
- ⇒ S37 – using numeracy
- ⇒ S17, S19 – developing children's health, safety, physical, social, emotional and behavioural skills

Meeting the Ofsted Welfare Regulations

Suitable people

Being an EYP means that you will hold responsibility for meeting the Ofsted statutory welfare requirements, you must ensure that adults looking after children, or having unsupervised access to them, are suitable to do so, and they must have appropriate qualifications, training, skills and knowledge. Staffing arrangements must be organized to ensure safety and to meet the needs of the children.

The leadership style that you adopt will impact on the culture and ethos of your setting – while you may need to become task-focused in order to meet Ofsted requirements, you may also need to focus on work relationships to gain your colleagues' support. Rodd (2006: 39) suggests that task performance and working relationships '… must operate simultaneously to effect efficient progress at work whilst building moral'. As Ofsted inspection to some may be perceived as a stressful experience, the role of the EYP is to become the team cheerleader and a morale booster.

Point to Remember

'To get the best out of people, lead from the front – if you are there, you are visible and not afraid to be seen working hard; others will follow.' (Leighton, 2007: 101)

EYPs must proactively keep their working knowledge and understanding about the national and local, legal requirements, policies and guidance related to promoting children's well-being and health and safety up to date. EYPs will not only use this knowledge and understanding to inform their own practice but they will also employ an appropriate leadership style to influence and monitor their own practice and leadership and support of others. Chapter 3 will help you to develop your leadership point of view and Chapter 8 will help you to explore the characteristics required to be a leader.

♀♀♀♀   Leadership Activity

What decisions and appropriate actions have you taken safeguard and promote babies, toddlers and young children's:

✓ welfare
✓ good health and hygiene

✓   prevention of illnesses and the spread of infection
✓   good behaviour
✓   safety (to include setting visits, collecting, sleeping checks, etc.).

Look at the EYPS standards:

⟹ S3, S5, S4, S19

Meeting Ofsted: Suitable premises, environment and equipment

The physical play environment as well as the physical play equipment, for example large pieces of climbing apparatus, sand pits, bikes and trikes, home corners, etc., needs to be managed effectively within an early years setting. Safety checks are paramount and need to be carried out on a regular basis. EYPs will in their own practice and leadership and support of others ensure that risk assessments are undertaken on a regular basis, safety checks are done on equipment and the premises, the play and care areas are kept clean and fit for purpose and that appropriate equipment and resources are safe and accessible. The outdoor and indoor spaces, furniture, equipment and toys must be safe and suitable for their purpose.

Point to Remember

'The physical environment must be a safe place for children and adults. Health and safety regulations must be adhered to, with staff taking responsibility, checking the premises for hazards regularly and ensuring prompt action is taken where necessary.' (Neaum and Tallek, 2002: 72)

Look at the EYPS standards:

⟹ S12, S19

Meeting Ofsted: Organization requirement

Providers must plan and organize their systems to ensure that every child receives an enjoyable and challenging learning and development experience that is tailored to meet their individual needs. The knowledge and understanding that EYPs have developed through their graduate studies and their own practice will inform their ability to lead and support colleagues to plan, design and implement and evaluate weekly and daily routines and play activities. They must be flexible in their approach and meet the development needs of all babies, toddlers and young children in their setting, service or network.

Point to Remember

Supportive behaviour 'involves listening to people, providing support and encouragement for their efforts and then facilitating their involvement in problem solving and decision making.' (Blanchard et al., 2004: 46)

Look at the EYPS standard:

⇒ S9

Meeting Ofsted: Documentation requirement

As part of the EYP's role, you will influence, shape, contribute to, monitor and evaluate the records, policies and procedures required for the safe and efficient management of the settings.

As an EYP, your personal beliefs and value systems will inform your understanding about what constitutes effective practice (this will be explored further in Chapter 3). You will use your informed judgement to contribute to the setting's records, policies and procedures as required by Ofsted. Records, policies and procedures are used to inform the setting's approach to the care and learning of babies, toddlers and young children, and the ways in which other early years practitioners working within your setting will conduct themselves.

Reflective Activity

Consider the range of records, policies and procedures in your setting. Examples may include:

- ✓ achieving the five ECM outcomes
- ✓ the implementation of the EYFS
- ✓ babies' sleep and feeding procedures
- ✓ children's meals and snacks
- ✓ collecting children
- ✓ behaviour and bullying procedures
- ✓ children's assessment and observation records
- ✓ health and safety procedures
- ✓ child protection and safeguarding
- ✓ working in partnership with parents and carers.

Which ones have you:

- influenced?
- contributed ideas to?
- implemented?
- reviewed recently?

Look at the EYPS standard:

⇒ S35

Each Ofsted category has *specific legal duties* that are clearly stated within the EYFS documentation. These include, for example, the *Suitable People* requirement that 'all supervisors and managers must hold a full and relevant level 3 (as defined by the Children's Workforce Development Council (CWDC)) and half of all other staff must hold a full and relevant level 2 (as defined by CWDC)' (DCSF, 2008b p. 31).

Specific legal requirements are very detailed in relation to adult to child ratios and these impact not only on the numbers of staff that need to be employed but also provide more detail about the necessary qualifications.

Suitable Premises regulations include the requirements that 'in registered provision, providers must meet the following space requirements:

- children under two years – 3.5 m² per child
- children aged two – 2.5 m² per child
- children aged three to five years – 2.3 m² per child'.

EYPs must ensure that, so far as is reasonable, the facilities, equipment and access to the premises are suitable for children with disabilities. The premises must be for the sole use of the provision during the hours of operation. Wherever possible, there should be access to an outdoor play area, and this is the expected norm for providers. In provision, where outdoor play space cannot be provided, outings should be planned and taken on a daily basis (unless circumstances make this inappropriate, for example unsafe weather conditions).

Point to Remember

'Inspection frameworks are clear and transparent and serve to provide a form of quality assurance as measured against agreed and published standards and criteria, however, those standards and frameworks alone do not define the essence of quality as informed by research and as it is continually developed in practice'. (Nutbrown, 2006: 113)

In August 2007, Ofsted published a report, *Getting on Well: Enjoying, Achieving and Contributing*, that showed how 99 per cent of the 27,200 childcare providers inspected in 2006-07 were judged satisfactory or better at supporting children to achieve well, enjoy their learning and make a positive contribution. The report provides an insight into how they met Ofsted National Standards, contributed to the *Every Child Matters* outcomes and may provide useful guidance for EYPS in planning childcare with knowledge about provision that Ofsted judged to be good.

 Key Points

- ✓ Adopt a leadership style to suit the task team and situation.
- ✓ Keep yourself up to date with local and national policies and frameworks.
- ✓ Lead from the front, be visible and do not be afraid to be seen working hard.
- ✓ Be aware that leadership is linked to learning.
- ✓ Deploy strong communication and interpersonal skills.
- ✓ Be observant of time management.
- ✓ Set yourself Smart Goals.
- ✓ Empower others.
- ✓ Listen to people, providing support and encouragement for their efforts and then facilitate their involvement in problem solving and decision making.
- ✓ Strive for continuous improvement.

Further Reading

Baldock, P., Fitzgerald, D. and Kay, J. (2005) *Understanding Early Years Policy*. London: Paul Chapman Publishing.

Nurse, A.D. (2007) *The New Early Years Professional*. Oxen: Routledge.

Rodd, J. (2006) *Leadership in Early Childhood*, 3rd edition. Maidenhead: Open University Press.

Useful Websites

Every Child Matters – www.everychildmatters.gov.uk/earlyyears/tenyearstrategy
Ofsted – www.ofsted.gov.uk
Statutory Framework for the Early Years Foundation Stage – www.standards. dcsf.gov.uk/
Sure Start – www.surestart.gov.uk
Early Support – www.earlysupport.org.uk

CHAPTER 2

WHAT IS THE EYPS PROCESS?

This chapter will provide an introduction to the format of the EYPS process – it is necessary to consider this at the beginning of the book in order to provide an overview of what the expectations are for those seeking the award of EYPS. This chapter will explain the CWDC (2008a) process for the formative assessment called the Gateway Review and the summative assessment process of the Written Tasks and Setting Visit. Links will be made to Chapter 9, 'Going through the Gateway'. This chapter will be further strengthened by the addition of supporting theory, case studies and reflective tasks. By starting to explore the concept of the early years leader in the context of both organizational and educational literature, theory and key research findings, the chapter aims to provide a starting point about the characteristics required by an EYP leading high-quality early years provision. The chapter challenges and explores leadership theory within the confines of a mainly female dominated workforce and opens up a debate about defining the characteristics required of the Early Years Leader today. The chapter concludes by asking the reader to explore their personal leadership perspective.

Starting the EYPS Journey

This book has been designed to support your journey to becoming an EYP, however, in order for you to make the most out of your journey and make it a positive experience, you will need to consider how you will balance your work commitments with your studies and your personal life. There will be demands on your time as for part of the training process which has been designed by CWDC (2008a) you will be required to attend training days with a CWDC-approved training provider, engage in periods of reflection, undertake a range of professional development activities, and engage in a non-traditional academic assessment process.

Overview of the EYPS Process

To achieve EYPS, you will be required to demonstrate that you are leading, managing and delivering effective practice in line with the set of 39 CWDC National Standards (CWDC, 2008b: Appendix 1). The standards are designed around working safely with babies, toddlers and young children from birth to five years and relate to the Early Years Foundation Stage.

The CWDC (2006) has designed a number of pathways for those aspiring to become an EYP:

- The four-month Validation Pathway is for candidates who already have considerable knowledge, experience and skills relative to the CWDC (2008a) EYPS standards.
- The six-month Short Extended Professional Development (EPD) Pathway is for early years professionals who have qualification and experience that is broadly relevant to EYPS but who require further training or experience to meet the standards.
- The fifteen-month Long Extended Professional Development (EPD) Pathway is for early years professionals who have qualification and experience that is broadly relevant to EYPS but who require training or experience to meet the standards, or for candidates that hold a relevant foundation degree who will be given the opportunity to top this up to a degree status with EYPS.
- The twelve-month Full Training Pathway is for graduates who are new to the early years – they will be given the opportunity to develop their knowledge, skills and understanding of working with babies, toddlers and young children. They will undertake full-time study and work experience in order to prepare them for a career in the early years sector.
- CWDC are also running a number of pilots for those currently studying on Foundation Degree and BA (hons) Early Years programmes and for those with an NVQ level 3 (or equivalent) qualification.

Table 2.1 *CWDC (2006) EYPS entry requirements*

For the Validation Pathway (4 months), Short Extended Professional Devlopment Pathway (6 months) and Long Extended Professional Development Pathway (15 months), you need to:

✓ work in full daycare or sessional settings
✓ be a childminder or childminding network leader
✓ be an early years professional involved in education and training for the early years workforce
✓ be an early years professional working for the Local Authority advisory services working with early years providers
✓ have a full degree or equivalent qualification (Level 6)
✓ have GCSE English and Maths (A–C) or a recognized equivalent
✓ be mentally and physically fit to work
✓ have a current CRB clearance
✓ have good communication skills
✓ have appropriate experience of working with babies, toddlers and young children from birth to the end of the Foundation Stage.

With the exception of the EYPS Full Training Pathway (CWDC, 2006), which will give candidates seeking a career in the early years sector the opportunity to undertake work experience, early years practitioners on the Validation Pathway (4 months), the Short Extended Professional Development Pathway (6 months) or the Long Extended Professional Development Pathway (15 months) will need to meet the criteria set by CWDC (2006) that is illustrated in Table 2.1.

The validation process that leads up to the award of EYPS is the same for whichever pathway you are following. Please see Figure 2.1 which describes the overall validation process and the training that you will receive to support you. By the time that you are ready to undertake your final assessment, you will be required to demonstrate your knowledge and understanding in relation to the EYPS standards and that you use this to inform your leadership of others and your own practice. Your training provider will provide you with a copy of the CWDC (2008a) *Candidate Handbook*. This will provide you with information about the programme.

You may be a graduate new to the profession, you may be working singly as a childminder or as part of a network of childminders, you may be working in a pre-school group or a group of small nurseries, you may be working in a Children's Centre or a day nursery, nonetheless, you will have certain attributes that will distinguish your role – whatever your circumstances, you will need to show, firstly, that you are a reflective practitioner and, secondly, that you are able to provide leadership and support to your colleagues in order to effect change and improvement in children's care and learning experiences (CWDC, 2008a).

Firstly, and most importantly, to be an EYP and to lead effective early years practice, you do not have to be in a senior position, a head of a setting or an organization. I have been privileged to work with some outstanding early years leaders from across the early years sector: childminding network coordinators, childminders, early years setting supervisors, room leaders, key workers, Special Education Needs Coordinators

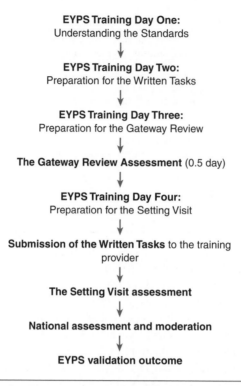

EYPS Training Day One:
Understanding the Standards
↓
EYPS Training Day Two:
Preparation for the Written Tasks
↓
EYPS Training Day Three:
Preparation for the Gateway Review
↓
The Gateway Review Assessment (0.5 day)
↓
EYPS Training Day Four:
Preparation for the Setting Visit
↓
Submission of the Written Tasks to the training
provider
↓
The Setting Visit assessment
↓
National assessment and moderation
↓
EYPS validation outcome

Figure 2.1   *The overall EYPS candidate validation process*

 Points for Reflection

Time Management

✓ How long is your EYPS training pathway? Are you able to demonstrate all of the CWDC criteria?

✓ Are there any areas that you will need to develop?

✓ Do you need to set yourself any Sustainable, Measurable, Achievable, Realistic and Time-focused (SMART) goals?

✓ Consider the time frame that you have to achieve the EYP status, look at the time that you have available, be realistic about your work and personal commitments – how are you going to manage yourself and your time?

✓ Do you need to make colleagues, friends or family aware that you are training to become an EYP and that you will need time to reflect, write and undertake some professional development activities?

EYPS candidate reviewing CWDC guidance

(SENCOs), Children's Centre coordinators, play workers, family liaison officers, university and Further Education early years lecturers, assessors and mentors, specialist support advisors, and early years advisors. So being an Early Years Leader is not about position – it is more about what you do and the way that you do it.

Point to Remember

Remember, 'Goals energise people. Specific, clear, challenging goals lead to greater effort and achievement than easy or vague goals'. (Blanchard, 2007: 144)

The Assessment Process

You will engage in three different types of assessment processes on your programme – these will include the:

- Gateway Review
- Written Tasks
- Setting Visit.

In Chapter 9, 'Going through the Gateway', I will be inviting you to explore the ways in which you can demonstrate your knowledge, skills and understanding for each of the assessments that you will be required to undertake.

The Gateway Review

Once you are ready to undertake your first assessment, your training provider will arrange for you to take part in a 'Gateway Review of Skills'. The analogy of a 'gateway' means that once you have successfully completed the assessment, you can go through the 'Gateway' and start your next stage of assessment. The Gateway Review does not contribute to your final assessment, however it can be used by your training provider to refer you on to a different pathway. The CWDC *Candidate Handbook* (2008a: 6–8) provides information about what is expected of you during the Gateway Review assessment.

The Gateway Review will last for half a day and you will be invited to attend your assessment centre to undertake a review of your skills. During the review, you will be asked to undertake written exercises, a personal interview, a group exercise, an interview with an actor and a written reflection alongside other candidates. The exercises are designed by CWDC to assess the knowledge, skills and understanding about what they consider fundamental to your training as an EYP. You will receive formative feedback from your Gateway Review, identifying your areas of strength and some development points to be considered. You may want to discuss these with your tutor or mentor. Table 2.2 describes the purpose of the CWDC Gateway Review.

The Written Tasks

During the last three months of whichever pathway you are following, you will be asked by your training provider to submit a series of reflective accounts of aspects of your own practice and experience of leading others. The written accounts must be written at graduate level and provide information abut how you lead and support other practitioners to implement the EYFS with babies, toddlers and young children. You will need to cross-reference your accounts to the CWDC EYPS standards (2008b). The Written Tasks must also reflect a depth and breadth of the knowledge and understanding that you have of the early years sector and how this underpins your practice. You will also be asked to collate a file of supporting documentary evidence, for example assessment records,

Table 2.2   *The GATEWAY process*

The overall GATEWAY process is designed, first, to check that you understand the standards and, second, to assess three skills generic to working as an EYP and fundamental to meeting the standards.

The three generic skills assessed in the Gateway Review:

1. *The ability to make decisions on the basis of sound judgement* *(see Chapter 8)*

- thinks beyond the immediate problem and avoids 'quick fix' solutions
- concentrates on what is most important
- makes appropriate decisions, using the available information but seeking further information when necessary
- bases decisions on agreed principles and policies.

2. *The ability to lead and support others* *(see Chapter 8)*

- gets ideas agreed, whether one's own or those of others
- improves practice by motivating others to achieve agreed aims
- recognizes and develops the potential of others
- proposes clear strategies for improvement as a change agent.

3. *The ability to relate to, and communicate with, others* *(see Chapters 7 and 8)*

- communicates clearly, both orally and in writing
- listens to others' concerns and responds appropriately
- shows respect for others in a sensitive manner
- manages own feelings and needs.

Adapted from CWDC *Candidate Handbook* (2008a)

plans, minutes of meetings, case studies, policies, etc. You must ensure confidentiality for the materials produced by deleting names and gaining written permission if you are using photographs. I always advise my candidates to annotate each piece of evidence by giving an overview of what their contribution was to each of the pieces of evidence, as you do not want to leave your assessor guessing – they only have a limited time to review your documentary evidence during the visit. As the Written Tasks and the documentary evidence file will form the basis of the next stage of your assessment – the 'Setting Visit' – they are very important documents and you must apportion time appropriately to ensure that you present yourself in the best way possible. It's a bit like imagining a TV talent show – 'You can be that EYP' – you must be able to demonstrate to your assessor how you can meet the EYPS standards.

The Setting Visit

I feel that this final stage of your assessment should be called the 'Setting Assessment', as a visit conjures up a picture of me visiting your setting to admire the children and the activities that are taking place and at the same time meet up with your colleagues and exchanging pleasantries. The Setting Visit is far more formal than this – your assessor will be working very hard, almost like a detective, to verify the claims that you have made against the standards in your written tasks. You will be interviewed by your assessor and you will be asked to show your assessor your file of supporting documentary evidence. You will take your assessor on a tour of your setting and you will arrange for a number of witnesses to either come into your setting to be interviewed by the assessor, or to be contacted during the day by telephone. The CWDC *Candidate Handbook* (2008a: 12–17) provides information about what is expected of you during the Setting Visit.

Defining the Early Years Professional

The CWDC define Early Years Professional (EYP) as someone who is a 'change agent and an innovator' (CWDC, 2008a). These words sound very grand and they have serious implications, and this description of an EYP might sound to you like an alien in a science fiction book. In reality, an EYP is the equivalent of an early years 'super hero' – the government in England has high expectations and believes that EYPs will make the government's early years transformation agenda happen. What does all this mean for you? This book will aid the journey in the search of the most appropriate leadership styles, characteristics and skills required to lead others, and at the same time guide you through ways of reflecting on the most appropriate way to meet the 39 CWDC EYPS National Standards (2008b: Appendix 1).

Throughout the book and during your EYPS training programme, you will be encouraged to be a 'reflective practitioner' and identify your personal leadership strengths, and at the same time consider ways in which you can strengthen and develop yourself as a Professional Early Years Leader.

 Points for Reflection

✓ What does raising the quality of the early years provision mean to you?
✓ What personal skills will you need to raise the quality of early years provision in your work place?
✓ How do you identify what colleagues know and can do?
✓ How do you manage change in the work place?
✓ How do you get others to take your ideas on board?

It seems so easy to refer to EYPS as a vehicle for change and one that will create transformational leaders. There lies a dichotomy – in as much as EYPs work in various roles across the public, voluntary and independent (PVI) sector, many hold responsibility for running their own business, many work for non-profit-making settings and others work within the Local Authority, and yet they are all equally responsible for delivering government policy and reforms.

> Leaders in early years settings which are very diverse in character as well as quality and effectiveness are henceforward charged with managing the related areas of care, health and family support and integrating these with education; they will also need to continue effectively to manage, deploy and develop staff with different professional perspectives and associated qualifications, as well as with varying levels of experience and exposure to professional training. (Siraj-Blatchford and Manni, 2006: 3)

What Makes an Effective Early Years Leader?

Leadership is a serious business and it is universally acknowledged that 'despite its contemporary importance, there is no agreed definition of the concept of leadership (Bush and Middlewood, 2005: 4). Yukl (2002: 4–5) believes that the definition of leadership is arbitrary and very subjective. Some definitions are more useful than others, but there is no "correct" definition'. Cuban in Bush and Middlewood (2005: 4) links leadership with change – he suggests that 'by leadership I mean influencing other's actions in achieving desirable ends. Leaders are people who shape the goals, motivations, and actions of others. Frequently they initiate change to reach existing and new goals … Leadership … takes … much ingenuity, energy and skill'.

My own experience of leading multi-professional early years teams while working as Head of School in an FE college, leading early years practitioners in two full-day-care nurseries (one on each of the college sites) and working with early years practitioners as a Local Authority Early Years Advisory Teacher, prompted my search for the big question: 'What makes an effective Early Years Leader?'. I am continuing to ask myself this question with the introduction of EYPS, which gives me the opportunity to share my research, observations and experience and to re-frame the big question: 'What makes an effective EYP?'. The key early years leadership characteristics illustrated in Figure 2.2 are the ones that I have identified in pursuit of answering the big question: 'What makes an effective Early Years Leader?'. They should be viewed as a starting point and over time they will change to meet individual needs of EYPs working in the early years sector.

What are the characteristics that will be required of you to become an effective early years leader? Are the qualities that you will need any different to the qualities that are needed by leaders who run a political party or a successful business?

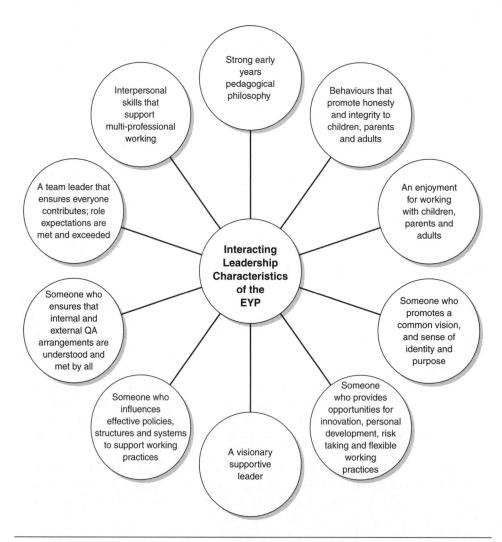

Figure 2.2   *Interacting leadership characteristics of the EYP*

Margaret Thatcher, the daughter of a shopkeeper, had the willpower to become Britain's first female Prime Minister at the age of 53. She possessed a strong vision and workable ideas to support it. She led Britain to a military victory over Argentina in 1982. She understood that politicians had to give military people clear orders about the ends and then leave them to get on with the means of doing it. Throughout the conflict, she portrayed leadership characteristics of courage, loyalty and perseverance and was admired for these throughout the world.

Nelson Mandela, despite serving 27 years in prison, played a leading role in the drive for peace in South Africa. He led the struggle to replace the apartheid regime of South Africa with a multi-racial democracy and became the first black South African President. He showed characteristics of immense courage, he stood by his personal moral code, he demonstrated a strong determination and is now a world-wide inspiration.

Sir Richard Branson set up the Virgin group in 1971 and is famous for being adventurous, innovative, having a sense of fun and a sense of competitive challenge. He aspires to delivering a quality service and believes in empowering his people and monitoring customer feedback to continually improve the customer's experience.

Like Sir Richard Branson, Sir Alan Sugar, who left school at the age of 16, has used his entrepreneurial business leadership skills to build up a large corporation. He portrays the leadership characteristics of having relentless energy, being a hard worker and needing a challenge. He sets himself new targets and doesn't suffer fools gladly. 'He is without doubt a born entrepreneur who trusts his finely tuned instincts and he has no time for focus groups, management gobbledygook or decision by committee. He has created a business by leading his people to the company vision and sustaining a team-based culture' (Brunel University, 2008).

Point for Reflection

Do you identify with any of the leadership values and characteristics portrayed by Margaret Thatcher, Nelson Mandela, Sir Richard Branson or Sir Alan Sugar?

In the quest to determine the leadership characteristics required of the EYP, let us now consider the leadership characteristics of the Early Years pioneers such as Dr Maria Montessori, Rudolf Steiner and Margaret McMillan. Are they any different to those offered by Margaret Thatcher, Nelson Mandela, Sir Richard Branson or Sir Alan Sugar?

The Montessori Nursery School organization was set up by Dr Maria Montessori in 1929 and is still in existence today. Its aim is to maintain and further develop Montessori ideas and principles for the full development of the human being (Montessori Society AMI, 2008). Fundamental to the Montessori approach is a great respect for the child as an individual. Professionals are trained and supported to develop an understanding about the ways to provide effective early years experiences that are respectful of the child's capabilities and level of needs, and yet at the same time challenge and develop a sense of awe and wonder. As a leader, Dr Maria Montessori was a visionary and her legacy is still recognized today. She held a strong sense of identity and a belief about how children should be educated and made this become a reality – she inspired others and recognized the importance of training and continuous professional development.

Rudolf Steiner also held a strong belief that education should be designed to meet the changing needs of a child as they develop physically, mentally and emotionally. He believed that it should help a child to fulfill their full potential but he did not believe in pushing children towards goals that adults or society in general believed to be desirable. Rudolf Steiner's leadership characteristics could be described as him being an idealist, a pragmatist, being proactive, being collaborative. He trained school teachers, he supervised the conversion of the school buildings, he met the parents, he got to know the children, he attended the teachers' meetings, he lectured and he attended lessons. 'Rudolf Steiner was always a charismatic figure, possessed by a burning energy and a formidable intellect' (Freedom in Education, 2008).

Margaret McMillan (1860–1931) worked with her sister Rachel in Bradford to try to improve the physical and intellectual welfare of slum children. In 1892, Margaret joined Dr James Kerr, Bradford's school medical officer, to carry out the first medical inspection of elementary school children in Britain. Kerr and McMillan published a report on the medical problems that they found and began a campaign to improve the health of children by arguing that local authorities should install bathrooms, improve ventilation and supply free school meals. Just like the other early years visionaries, Margaret Macmillan stood by her strong conviction, campaigned for her cause and made things happen.

Leadership and the Early Years Workforce

The ELEYS study (Siraj-Blatchford and Manni, 2006: 13) identifies that the early years workforce in Britain is predominately female: 'The Daycare Trust reports that 97.5% of the childcare workforce is female. Yet much of the current literature on leadership and management has ignored issues of gender and much of the literature and research in the wider context of education has inevitably [sic] been based upon men's experiences and male approaches. Cubillo (1999) argues that "the modes on which the characteristics of effective leaders are based are therefore stereotypically androcentric", often associated with "masculine" attributes and behaviours such as competitiveness, dynamism, power and agressivity.'

I agree with this statement and discovered whilst undertaking my Masters-level study in Educational Leadership that most of the literature surrounding leadership has been written for corporate organizations by males often described as 'leadership gurus'. These include Charles Handy, Stephen Covey, Ken Blanchard, Warren Bennis, John Kotter and Peter Senge, amongst others. Their leadership, theories, tools, frameworks and models are aimed at corporate business leaders, however they are acknowledged in educational circles and provide a valuable insight into the mystical world of leadership. There is a National College for School Leadership and literature has been written to support school leaders – maybe one day we will have a National College for Early Years Leaders. Bolam (1999: 194) in Bush and Middlewood (2005) defines school leaders as taking on '… the responsibility for policy formation and, where appropriate, organisational transformation', which in my mind, compares favourably to the exciting new role of the EYP.

Point for Reflection

You do not have to be perfect to lead effective early years practice.

'There has been a long search for the alchemy of Leadership: we all want to find the elusive pixie dust that we can sprinkle on ourselves to turn us into glittering leaders.' (Owen, 2005: xii)

Point for Reflection

'One of the dangers for women is that they're often seen as the ones who take care of an organisation. They are perceived to have the caring skills of empathy, or being good with people or being good listeners. Male leaders are seen as very incisive people who can take charge and make decisions. This whole 'taking care' versus 'taking charge' thing is very stereotypical and can disadvantage women when it comes to talking about Leadership. Actually I think a leader has to have both traits. You have to be caring as a leader and humane, you have to demonstrate trust and authenticity. But you have to take charge, pull teams together and unify them behind a common purpose.' (Carolyn McCall, chair of Opportunity Now, which works for gender equality and diversity in the work place – Leighton, 2007: 239)

Consider the following questions:

✓ Can you identify a time when you had to take charge, pull people together and unify them?
✓ How did you achieve this?
✓ What did you learn from the experience?

Look at the EYPS standards:

⇒ S33, S34, S36

In the past, lack of opportunities for Early Years Leadership training coupled with limited access to experienced role models (Humphries and Sendon, 2000; Ebeck and Waniganayake, 2003 in Rodd, 2006: 23) and the antithesis many women appear to have towards roles that involve power and authority (Cox, 1996 in Rodd, 2006: 23) have acted to impede development of an understanding of leadership, particularly as it pertains to early childhood. As Belenky et al. (1986) in Siraj-Blatchford and Manni (2006: 12) put it: 'Until recently women have played only a minor role as theorists in the social sciences. The omission of women from scientific studies is almost universally ignored when scientists draw conclusions from their findings and generalise what they have learned from the study of men. If and when scientists turn to the study of women, they typically look for ways in which women conform or diverge from patterns found in the study of men'.

Arguably, much of the existing literature on early years leadership to support EYPS needs to be reviewed with an element of caution, as it can be perceived as excessively prescriptive, disregarding the differences that exist between corporate organizations and the wide range of early years services EYPs are working within.

It was within these challenging contexts that the Effective Leadership in the Early Years Sector (ELEYS) study (Siraj-Blatchford and Manni, 2006) was developed as an extension of the Researching Effective Pedagogy in the Early Years (REPEY) study (Siraj-Blatchford et al., 2002).

The ELEYS research (2006: 5) was designed to explore the following questions:

- To what extent does literature and research tell us about effective educational leadership in the early years sector?
- What characteristics or patterns of leadership can be identified in the REPEY sample of effective settings?

The emininent researchers undertaking the literature review for the ELEYS study reported that 'Due to the paucity of evidence-based (i.e. non-anecdotal) literature that is available related to the leadership and management of early years settings, the authors were forced to consult leadership and management literature associated with both primary and secondary schools'. While this literature provided a starting point for their study, it was 'treated with special caution and applied only where they are considered particularly relevant to the early years contexts' (Siraj-Blatchford and Manni, 2006).

The lack of literature relating to Early Years Leadership identified in the ELEYS study makes the journey to EYPS open-ended and exciting. To this purpose, while there will be reference made throughout this book to a number of respected early years authors, theorists, researchers and government guides, reference will also be made to a range of literature produced by non-early years authorities. You will need to research and explore materials that will work best for you.

Points for Reflection

Look at the ELEYS study:

- ✓ Consider each category.
- ✓ How confident are you in each category?
- ✓ Do you need further training in any category?
- ✓ Which categories do you feel confident about?
- ✓ Can you find any evidence to support categories that you feel confident about?

ELEYS 'categories of effective leadership practice':	Look at the EYPS standards:
Identifying and articulating a collective vision, especially with regard to pedagogy and curriculum	⇒ S1
Ensuring shared understandings, meanings and goals: building common purposes	⇒ S33
Effective communication: providing a level of *transparency* in regard to expectations, practices and processes	⇒ S34
Encouraging reflection: which acts as an impetus for change and the motivation for ongoing learning and development	⇒ S38
Commitment to ongoing, professional development: supporting staff to become more critically reflective in their practice	⇒ S38
Monitoring and assessing practice: through collaborative dialogue and action research	⇒ S10
Building a learning community and team culture: establishing a community of learners	⇒ S39
Encouraging and facilitating parent and community partnerships: promoting achievement for all young children	⇒ S31

Being an Early Years Leader requires you to utilize your many talents. If we reflect on the work of the early years pioneers, Dr Maria Montessori, Rudolf Steiner and Margaret McMillan, the political leaders Margaret Thatcher and Nelson Mandela and the business leaders Sir Richard Branson or Sir Alan Sugar, the things they all have in common are a strong vision, inspirational leadership and a willingness to put all of themselves into their roles. As an EYP, you will be asked to stand up for what is important, and adapt your ways of working appropriately to meet new challenges. To be an EYP, you will need to be emotionally intelligent and self-aware, and know your own strengths and limitations. You will develop both children's and your colleagues' learning and at the same time sustain a culture of mutual respect and collaborative working. You will need to build a platform for long-term success, by inspiring others, supporting their needs and guiding them through complex situations to collaborative decisions. In short, you will need to be committed to being an early years 'super hero' and become a key player in the British government's agenda in raising the quality of early years education.

To be an effective leader, it is important that you are clear about your thoughts on leadership. You need to be able to communicate these to your colleagues, your EYPS training provider, your EYPS mentor and your EYPS assessors, parents, carers and any other agencies that you work with. This will help others understand where you are coming from and will also help to clarify what they can expect from you and what you will expect from them. To help you establish a personal Early Years Leadership perspective, please complete the activity below.

Reflective Activity

What is your early years leadership perspective?

To clarify your EYP leadership perspective and to help you explain it to others, do the activities below:

1. List the leaders that have influenced you, such as parents, teachers, colleagues, politicians and sports people and note how they have inspired you.
2. Write a brief definition of yourself, your life, your work, why you are training for EYPS, what you are doing, how you model effective practice to others, what you are aspiring to.
3. List some personal characteristics that make you feel good about yourself, such as innovative, friendly, proactive, flexible, reliable, child-centred, people-oriented, trustworthy, caring.
4. list what others can expect of you as an EYP, for example offer inspiration, make informed decisions, set challenging goals and targets, encourage open communication, develop others.
5. List what you expect of others, for example to accept responsibility, a willingness to view change as positive, effective practice, strong relationships with children, parents and carers, good team-working and collaborative skills, a commitment to continuous professional development.
6. To discover your leadership perspective, combine the definition of yourself with two of the personal characteristics that make you feel good about yourself, two things that you think others can expect of you and two things that you expect of others .

Table 2.3 *Definitions of 'leading effective practice' from the Leading Effective Practice workshop held at the South East Region EYPS 'Here to Stay' Conference 2008*

Reflective and enthusiastic, offers inspiration and is approachable. Is valued and respected, and is open to change.

(Baby Room Leader)

To have a positive outlook. To go on a learning journey. Passionate about early years, dedicated to making a difference for children and families.

(Coordinator and Early Years Consultant)

Create children who believe they can achieve.

(Strategy Manager)

To be a change agent. A reflective practitioner who desires to empower children and instill a love of life-long learning.

(Manager and Head of Nursey)

An influential role model committed to raising standards of early years through sustained shared thinking and child-centred reflective practice.

(Family Services Manager, Room Supervisor, Deputy Manager and Nursery Manager)

Being a role model, aspiring to be like other leaders.

(Nursery Nurse)

Parents have faith in you. Children have enthusiasm. Faith in your abilities and inspiration.

(Manager and Nursery Nurse)

Adaptable, flexible and positive.

(Childcare Centre Manager)

Practice should be child-centred and all staff valued and given responsibilities. To be fair and consistent. Only expect from others what you would do yourself.

(Head of Nursing)

We know we can make a difference.

(Deputy Supervisor)

An inspirational agent for change.

(Leadership Practitioner)

Leadership is about being self-motivated, being an enthusiastic person with effective communication skills, inspiring others to work together to a shared vision, and take the team on a continuous journey.

(Day Nursery Manager)

A good listener who is able to learn from others.

(Trainee EYP)

Raise standards, be a good communicator, caring and warm, passionate, energetic, have empathy, make informed decisions. Be knowledgeable and understanding. Willingly do dirty jobs. Give approval and support.

(Children's Centre Manager)

Finally, to make your EYPS journey a successful one, you must aim to reflect on your own practice and the leadership and support that you give to your colleagues in your early years setting, network or service. To do this, I urge you to do two things: firstly, aim to keep a reflective log from the outset of your programme and, secondly, start to collate any documents that you feel demonstrate your practice against the EYPS standards, for example plans, routines, reports, observations, records of contact with parents and audits of resources. This will help you prepare for your EYPS assessments (more information about these can be found in Chapters 9, 10 and 11). Allow yourself time to engage in reflective thinking, and use your reflective log to keep notes of ideas that you have had, and incidents and activities that you have had to lead or think on your feet about. Your reflective log will give you an insight into how you feel about your role. It will highlight your anxieties and uncertainties and give you the opportunity to reflect on solution-focused practice.

While recording your reflective log, consider:

- your personal feelings about leading effective practice with babies, toddlers and young children
- what worked well and what didn't work so well when trying to motivate others
- what research, theory, policy and literature relates to your personal experience
- the benefits and outcomes for the children (aged 0–5 years) and their families
- your personal learning of the situation or event.

Your log will help you to prepare for the Gateway Review assessment and the Setting Visit assessment. Further reference to the reflective log can be found in Chapter 3.

 Key Points

✓ Become a 'reflective leader'.
✓ Consider that to be a leader, you do not have to be in a senior position, a head of a setting or an organization.
✓ Remember that being an Early Years Leader is not about position – it is more about what you do and the way that you do it.
✓ Set goals that lead to greater effort and achievement rather than easy or vague ones.
✓ Continually reflect on and evaluate your leadership training needs.
✓ Establish a personal 'Early Years Leadership' perspective and share it with your colleagues, parents and carers and your EYPS training provider.
✓ Keep a journal to record your thoughts, your research and reading as you go through the process.

Further Reading

Owen, J. (2005) *How to Lead*. Harlow: Pearson Education.
Rodd, J. (2006) 'Unpicking leadership in the early childhood context', in *Leadership in Early Childhood*, 3rd edition. Maidenhead: Open University Press.
Whalley, M.E. (2008) *Leading Practice in Early Years Settings*. Exeter: Learning Matters.

Useful Websites

Children's Workforce Development Council – www.cwdccouncil.org.uk
Effective Leadership in the Early Years Sector (ELEYS) study (Siraj-Blatchford and Manni, 2006) – www.gtce.org.uk/shared/contentlibs/126795/93128/120213/eleys_study.pdf
Researching Effective Pedagogy in the Early Years (REPEY) study (Siraj-Blatchford et al., 2002) – www.dfes.gov.uk/research/data/uploadfiles/RR356.pdf

CHAPTER 3

WHAT QUALITIES, KNOWLEDGE, SKILLS AND UNDERSTANDING DOES AN EYP NEED TO HAVE?

This chapter will explore the knowledge and understanding that is identified in the 39 EYPS National Standards (CWDC, 2008b) and the expectation that they will underpin the EYP's ability to lead, model and establish ways to put the standards into practice. While Chapter 2 invited you to explore a range of leadership characteristics that are related to the role of the EYP, this chapter invites you to reflect on and interpret those leadership characteristics in relation to the ways in which you lead and support others and role-model effective practice within the context of the 39 CWDC National Standards.

This chapter also draws your attention to the importance of being a reflective practitioner within the context of developing a strong self-awareness about your own practice and your abilities to lead and support others.

Your knowledge, skills and understanding about early years practice will have been developed as a consequence of leading the delivery of the Early Years Foundation Stage (EYFS), as part of any research and training that you have undertaken as part of your degree-level studies or within your wider professional role. Your graduate-level studies will have introduced you to the graduate-level skills of review, analysis, critique and evaluation which no doubt you will have continued to use in your exploration of the wide range of early years literature, research, policies and documents that have been written as a consequence of the government's early years workforce reforms arising from *Every Child Matters* (DfES, 2003b) and the introduction of the EYFS (2008).

This is endorsed by CWDC who suggest that:

> As post-graduates, the depth and breadth of EYPs' knowledge and understanding enable them to practise and model practice at a high level and to reflect upon their own practice in order to effect continuous improvement. Their personal practice, and their leadership and support of colleagues, are rooted in a secure grasp of important sources such as national policy, statutory and non-statutory frameworks and guidance, and research on child development and early years practice. Thus informed, EYPs can explain to colleagues and parents the rationale for policy, practice and improvement. (CWDC: 2008b)

Chapter 2 discussed the concept of the EYP being the government's aspirational change agent, an innovator and a super hero, key to raising the quality of early years provision. These aspirations require you to be an outstanding leader, an exceptional practitioner, a cheer leader and a visionary – no pressure here then! To fulfil this, you will need to demonstrate how you can work skilfully with others and in doing this you will need to consider how to:

✓ create strong teams
✓ be a good role model
✓ became emotionally intelligent
✓ be a good listener
✓ be a mentor
✓ be intuitive about others' capabilities
✓ be sensitive to others' needs
✓ be focused
✓ be able to develop others
✓ be able to support others during periods of change.

While the CWDC EYPS standards cover the generic qualities, skills, knowledge and understanding required of the EYP, it must be acknowledged that there is a diverse range of leadership roles, organizational differences and social contexts within which the childcare workforce operates.

For some, you may be leading effective early years practice working within:

• full daycare
• a crèche
• a Children's Centre
• a childminding network
• a Local Authority advisory team

- Further Education
- a private, voluntary or independent setting.

The leadership qualities and characteristics that you demonstrate will very much depend on your job role, the setting or organization that you are based in and the social context in which your provision is located. Embarking on the EYPS journey may require further learning, training and professional development for some of you. It is important that you identify your personal training needs and seek professional training either from your training provider or through your Local Authority Early Years unit, for example you may need further training on managing change, developing effective teams or researching ways to use emotional intelligence.

 Points for Reflection

Emotional intelligence – the ability to identify and respond sensitively to one's own and others' feelings (Goleman, 1996)

Critical thinking – the ability to influence others through logical and analytical reasoning

Directional clarity – the ability to set, articulate and motivate people to commit to clear goals

Creative intelligence – the ability to solve problems by integrating and applying knowledge and understanding of skills

People enablement – the ability to empower people by offering support and mentoring

Reciprocal communication – the ability to listen empathetically and to network with others

Change orchestration – the ability to lead change proactively and constructively

Perseverance – the capacity to behave assertively, confidently and professionally

Source: Rodd, 2006: 61

Look at the EYPS standards:

⇒ S33, S34, S36, S39

Reflective Practice

As discussed in Chapter 2, to start your EYPS reflective journey, you will need to set some time aside for yourself to reflect, review, analyze, evaluate and record the range of leadership experiences that you have had in your own setting or in other settings or in a network.

> The cycle of informed reflection, self-evaluation and development that lies at the heart of this process takes openness and the capacity to step back and look at your pratice with absolute honesty – warts and all! This is not a question of superficially ticking the boxes but an altogether more demanding way of analysing what it is that you do. You will need to think in depth about those aspects of your practice that are effective and why, checking that there is evidence to support the judgements that you have made. You will also need to explore the elements that are less successful and challenge yourself to make improvements. (Bruce, 2006: 5)

Point for Reflection

'If you don't know where you are, your true situation, then you are lost from the outset. You cannot plot a course forward if you don't know where you are starting from.' (Sir Terry Leahy, Tesco, quoted in Leighton, 2007: 67)

To demonstrate that you are working at the high level required of an EYP, use your reflective log (discussed in Chapter 2) to reflect, review, analyze, critique and evaluate your experience of leading practice and working with the 0–5s against the CWDC EYPS National Standards (2000b). The standards set out what EYPs should know, understand and be able to do, both in their own practice and in their leadership and support of others.

The CWDC National Standards not only set out what will be expected of you, they also signpost the knowledge, skills, understanding and experience that you will need to have in working with babies, toddlers and young children from birth to the end of the EYFS. As you embark on your reflective journey against the CWDC EYPS National Standards, you will begin to identify the standards that you feel most confident about and that will help you to gather evidence to support the claim that you are making. For the standards that you are not feeling quite so confident about, you may want to consider setting yourself some appropriate SMART goals.

Essentially, when you set yourself some SMART goals, you will need to consider what it is you need to do, how you will make it happen, how you will organize it, who you will need to involve and finally when it needs to be done. Remember that you will need to constantly monitor and revise your goals in order for them to work for you.

Reflective Activity

SMART stands for:

S Specific
M Measurable
A Achievable
R Realistic
T Time-constrained

To help you identify some **SMART** goals, answer the questions below:

✓ What are my training needs?
✓ Where and when is the training taking place?
✓ Do I need to organize any placement experience?
✓ What research, policies, documents, frameworks or reports do I need to review?
✓ Do I need to undertake any work experience working with babies, toddlers or young children or a combination of age ranges?
✓ How will I organize my time and my work commitments?
✓ Who do I need to keep informed?
✓ Do I need to arrange for someone to cover me in my absence?
✓ What time frame am I working in?

To help you identify what knowledge and understanding you have in relation to the CWDC EYPS standards, this chapter asks you to undertake a number of reflective activities designed around the 39 standards. The depth and breadth of your knowledge and understanding will change over the duration of the EYPS programme and you may wish to revisit these tasks to assess the progress that you have made or to prepare yourself for the first assessment, the Gateway Review, and the Setting Visit which takes place at the end of the programme. Further information about the CWDC EYPS National Standards can be found in the *Guidance to the Standards* (CWDC, 2008b) document, which sets out some of the characteristics of an EYP and some aspects of their role. It also introduces the EYP standards and provides guidance about how to interpret them and what they mean both for personal practice and the EYP's leadership and support of others.

When you engage in the reflective activities, try to identify practical examples to illustrate your experience as a leader. Consider the areas covered by the standards and how you put these into your own practice. Identify those areas that you will need to develop further. Now that you have reflected on EPPE (Sylva et al., 2004) and KEEP (DfES, 2005b) discussed in Chapter 1, you will have developed an appreciation as to why the areas addressed in the CWDC EYPS standards are so important. Try to reflect on your leadership experience against each of the standards, and at the same time, try to identify any documentary evidence that you have contributed to, as this can be used to support your preparation of the EYPS assessments.

The CWDC EYPS National Standards are organized into the following six areas:

- ✓ knowledge and understanding
- ✓ effective practice
- ✓ relationships with children
- ✓ communicating and working in partnership with families and carers
- ✓ team work and collaboration
- ✓ professional development.

This chapter aims to introduce you to the context of each of the six areas identified and they will be developed further in Chapters 4 to 8.

Knowledge and Understanding

The standards for Knowledge and Understanding identify the key areas of knowledge and understanding that you are expected to know. These also relate to the other EYPS standards which are concerned with your personal practice, your relationships with children, your partnership with parents and carers, your relationships with your colleagues and the professional development needs of both yourself and your colleagues.

Reflective Activity

EYP role and accountability:

1. Reflect on the questions.
2. Use your EYPS reflective log to record recent examples of your practice.
3. Identify documents to support your examples and keep them in a safe place.

⇒ S1

- ✓ What is your knowledge and understanding of the EYFS (DCSF, 2008b)?
- ✓ How do you put this in to your own practice?
- ✓ How do you communicate the content of the EYFS to your colleagues?

(Continued)

(Continued)

⇒ S2

✓ What is your knowledge and understanding of the broad developmental stages that children pass through from birth to the end of the foundation stage?

✓ What is your understanding about the ways that a child's development can be influenced by cultural and environmental factors?

✓ How do you ensure that colleagues take account of young children's developmental stages?

⇒ S3

✓ What is your knowledge and understanding about the transitions that all children aged 0–5 years pass through?

✓ How do you support others to develop an understanding about the effects that transitions can have on children's behaviour and learning?

⇒ S4

✓ What is your knowledge and understanding about the main provisions of national and local statutory and non-statutory frameworks?

✓ How do you ensure that the implications and responsibilities of the national and local statutory and non-statutory frameworks are followed in your setting?

✓ How do you develop your colleagues' understanding of the statutory and non-statutory frameworks?

⇒ S5

✓ What contribution can other professionals make to babies, toddlers and young children's physical and emotional well-being, learning and development needs?

✓ How do you develop your colleagues' understanding and ability to work collaboratively with other professionals within and beyond the setting?

⇒ S6

✓ What is your knowledge and understanding of the current legal requirements, national policies and guidance on health and safety, safeguarding and promoting the well-being of children?

✓ How do you demonstrate this knowledge and understanding within your own practice?

✓ How do you use this knowledge and understanding of the legal requirements, policies and guidance to support colleagues and influence their practice?

All the reflective questions above relate to the CWDC EYPS standards (2008b).

Effective Practice

The Effective Practice Standards are the largest set of standards as there are 18 EYPS standards for you to consider in this group. They relate to your own personal practice and the way that you lead and support your colleagues – you will be encouraged to explore these in more detail in Chapter 4. This set of standards asks you to reflect on the way that you lead:

- relationships with children
- communications and working in partnership with families and carers
- team work and collaboration
- professional development.

As mentioned previously, the review of the KEEP (DfES, 2005b) document that you undertook in Chapter 1 will help you to reflect on the multi-faceted nature of the EYP's role for the Effective Practice set of standards. These standards are concerned with the way in which you promote effective practice for babies, toddlers and young children's care, learning and well-being. For this set of standards, you will also need to consider how you promote children's rights and at the same time support and extend their learning within an inclusive environment.

Reflective Activity

The leadership characteristics that you adopt for this set of standards will very much depend on the type of setting that you are working in and the social–political context of the area in which your setting is situated.

1. Reflect on the questions.
2. Use your EYPS reflective log to record recent examples of your practice.
3. Identify documents to support your examples and keep them in a safe place.

Effective Practice 1		Look at the EYPS standards:
✓	What are your values and expectations and how do they underpin your own practice and your leadership of others?	⇒ S7

(Continued)

(Continued)

✓ How do you demonstrate in your own practice and leadership
of others how to: ⟹ S8

  • create stimulating environments, both indoors and   ⟹ S17
    outdoors
  • safeguard all children's welfare and respect their rights   ⟹ S19
  • promote positive behaviour strategies?   ⟹ S20

✓ How do you respect diversity and promote inclusion   ⟹ S12
across all the elements of your practice?   ⟹ S18

✓ How do you lead, plan and provide developmentally   ⟹ S9
appropriate activities and experiences for babies,   ⟹ S11
toddlers and young children?   ⟹ S12
                                                                    ⟹ S14
                                                                    ⟹ S15
                                                                    ⟹ S16

✓ How do you promote differentiated provision to meet   ⟹ S13
each individual child's need?   ⟹ S23

✓ How do you model and lead a culture of review and   ⟹ S10
take responsibility for individual children's well-being,   ⟹ S21
learning and development?   ⟹ S22
                                                                    ⟹ S24

(Based on the CWDC Guidance to the Standards (2008b))

The EPPE (Sylva et al., 2004) research and the ELEYS (Siraj-Blatchford and Manni, 2006) study complement the CWDC EYPS standards (2008b). Effective leadership in the early years is concerned with creating the right context to improve standards in teaching and learning and also fostering the belief that babies, toddlers, young children and their parents have the right to access high-quality early years services. You should also become a social entrepreneur whilst working with a strong value base, and be a well-informed thinker and able to engage in rigorous debate and reflection with a commitment to your own learning and the learning of the people that you lead (Whalley, 2005 in Nurse, 2007). Kathryn Solly, who calls herself Head Learner and Head Teacher of Chelsea Open Air Nursery, told EYPS at the first south-east region EYPS conference (2008) that the features of an early years leader are to be:

• adaptable
• energetic
• people-oriented

- quality-conscious
- unifying in style
- entrepreneurial
- focused
- informal and inclusive.

Reflective Activity

Effective Practice 2:

1. Reflect on the ways that you support your colleagues in your setting or in other settings or in a network.
2. Identify sources of documentary evidence that will support your Setting Visit assessment.

The sources of documentary evidence that you identify must be ones that you have contributed to, for example you may have briefing notes or draft policies, training documents, minutes of team or network meetings, room plans, resource inventories, etc.

How do you support your colleagues in your setting or in other settings or in a network to:

- ✓ undertake joint observations of babies, toddlers and young children in order to develop their skills in assessing individual children's needs and establishing the next steps in their learning and development?
- ✓ respect inclusive practice and diversity?
- ✓ deal with situations in which children or carers express inappropriate stereotypical viewpoints?
- ✓ undertake risk assessments?
- ✓ raise their level of practice?
- ✓ review existing resources in terms of their fitness-for-purpose?
- ✓ share good practice?
- ✓ make contributions to multi-professional planning and reviews?
- ✓ induct new colleagues to the setting or early years work?
- ✓ rearrange rooms/areas with a view to creating better use of the space or more opportunity for a specific activity, and evaluate the effect?
- ✓ convey messages about health and well-being to parents and carers?

Look at the EYPS standards:

⇒ S7–24

(Adapted from the CWDC Guidance to the Standards (2008b))

Relationships with Children

For the relationship with children group of standards (S25–28), you are invited to consider the ways in which you build and sustain a personal relationship with the babies, toddlers and young children that you work with (this area will be explored further in Chapter 5). The babies, toddlers and young children that you are responsible for can be within your own setting, service and network or any setting that you visit to undertake your work experience. You will need to show how you support the well-being, learning and development of these children within your leadership practice. You will also need to establish ways in which you expertly promote high standards of communication for all the babies, toddlers and young children and demonstrate how you promote an inclusive approach which takes account of the family and the child's background, culture and ability.

The CWDC (2008b) suggests that EYPs should appreciate that good relationships are characterized by not only talking with children and in making clear their expectations of them, but also listening to, valuing and respecting them. You will therefore be required to demonstrate how you develop and maintain relationships that are constructive and at the same time develop children's well-being, learning and development. As a graduate leader, you may have researched the work of Professor Dr Ferre Laevers of the Centre for Experiential Education, at the University of Leuvan in Belgium, who is widely known for his work on children's emotional well-being and involvement and how it can make a difference to their well-being, learning and development. His work will be explored further in Chapter 5.

Points for Reflection

Relationships with children:

1. Reflect on the ways that you support your colleagues in your setting or in other settings or in a network.
2. Identify sources of documentary evidence from this area that will support your Setting Visit assessment.

The sources of documentary evidence that you identify must be ones that you have contributed to, for example child communication briefing notes, child observations, planning documents, etc.

How do you support your colleagues in your setting or in other settings or in a network to:

✓ communicate with children with little or no speech or who have limited familiarity with the English language?

✓ use a range of methods, both verbal and non-verbal, to communicate effectively and sensitively with children?

✓ establish supportive and constructive relationships with children and treat them with fairness and respect?

✓ plan opportunities for your colleagues to observe, talk and listen to children?

✓ model personal skills in listening to and responding positively to children?

✓ encourage others to find out what interests children have at home or in the local community and encourage them to share them with other children, or use them as a starting point for a project?

✓ undertake joint observations, evaluate the child's development and plan for the next steps?

✓ communicate with children at child height?

✓ understand the benefit of listening to what children have to say?

✓ respond constructively to what children say?

✓ give appropriate feedback to children?

✓ listen to the babies, toddlers and young children and pay attention to what they have to say?

✓ value and respect the views of the babies, toddlers and young children?

Look at the EYPS standards:

⇒ S25–28

(Adapted from the CWDC Guidance to the Standards (2008b))

Communicating and Working in Partnership with Families and Carers

The EYPS National Standards (CWDC, 2008b) for communicating and working in partnership with families and carers suggest that young children do well when they experience a coherent approach at home and across all the settings in which they are cared for and educated. EYPs must be aware that the best outcomes for children are likely to be established when they lead practitioners to share their aims with parents and encourage them to become involved in their children's development and learning so that they can support those aims at home. Chapter 6 explores the ways to communicate and work effectively in partnership with parents in more depth. As a graduate and an EYP, you must show the ways in which you have developed a firm understanding about the ways in which the child's home background can impact on their learning, well-being and developmental needs. You will understand the importance of taking these into account when forming close relationships with the parents and carers. Equally

A practitioner discussing the child's progress with a parent at an EYP's setting

importantly, you will understand the necessity to develop and sustain a strong partnership approach between the home and the early years setting which is based on mutual respect.

As an EYP, you must also demonstrate your understanding about why it is so important to communicate effectively with parents/carers and exchange valuable information that can be used to inform the planning and practice of the setting. The range and type of information that you exchange includes children's allergies, likes and dislikes, their competence in language and communication at home, the standard of their behaviour, even their favourite toy! EYPs should have the knowledge to understand that discussions held with parents provide a basis for establishing a strong home and setting partnership. Once these are established, you can work together to support children's learning and development. As an advisory teacher, I often visited settings and saw bilingual signs and labels displayed around the setting. These very often had been produced by the EYP in consultation with a parent who spoke English as a second language. These signs were beautifully produced in their mother tongue and were used to support the children's learning.

EYPs will also need to show the ways in which they support parents who turn to them for advice, guidance and information about the best ways they can care for and educate their child. In my role as a Local Authority advisory teacher, I often supported early years practitioners to consider the best ways to offer guidance and support to parents on topics ranging from children's speech and language difficulties, reassuring parents about their child's age stage and level of development, informing parents about what can be expected from their child's transitions into school and ways in which to encourage healthy eating and healthy lifestyles. On occasions, I found myself advising practitioners about how to reach parents that were reluctant to come into the setting. Very often, I would attend meetings to explore the reasons why these parents and carers were hard to reach. The reasons varied between family pressures, bereavement in the family, English as a second language to single-parent mothers feeling isolated and not very confident about their parenting skills. As an EYP, you must be able to show how you listen to these types of parents'/carers' concerns in a sensitive manner using the emotional intelligence that we discussed earlier in this chapter. You must consider the best ways that you offer advice and guidance to motivate and encourage parents/carers to support the well-being and learning of their children at home. Sometimes this may involve you referring the parents to another organization or professional in order to support their needs.

Reflective Activity

Communicating and working in partnership with families and carers:

1. Reflect on the ways that you support your colleagues in your setting or in other settings or in a network.
2. Identify any sources of documentary evidence from this area that will support your Setting Visit assessment.

The sources of documentary evidence that you identify must be ones that you have contributed to, for example parents'/carers' policy documents, staff training and induction materials, parents'/carers' newsletters, child profiles, etc.

How do you support your colleagues in your setting or in other settings or in a network to:

- ✓ establish and sustain a welcoming atmosphere where parents feel able to exchange information about their child's well-being, learning and development?
- ✓ have arrangements in place to discuss with parents their child's well-being, progress and achievements?
- ✓ share information with parents on the well-being, learning and development of children in their care?
- ✓ recognize and value the contribution that parents can make to children's well-being, learning and development?
- ✓ work in partnership with families and carers?
- ✓ involve parents as active partners in their children's well-being, learning and development?
- ✓ lead and support colleagues in recognizing and making the most of the parents'/carers' contributions?

(Continued)

(Continued)

✓ develop and maintain positive, professional and respectful relationships with parents?

✓ demonstrate empathy, sensitivity and confidentiality when communicating with parents?

✓ establish and maintain positive and effective relationships with parents?

✓ take account of each child's home circumstances in order to identify any factors that might affect the child's learning and development?

✓ establish with parents an effective two-way flow of information about the child's learning experiences and development?

✓ recognize when parents need support in nurturing their children?

Look at the EYPS standards:

⇒ S29–32

(Adapted from the CWDC Guidance to the Standards (2008b))

Team Work and Collaboration

Unlike the other areas of standards which concentrate on the EYP's own practice with babies, toddlers and young children, the CWDC National Standards for team work and collaboration (S33–36) ask you to demonstrate the ways in which you use your professional leadership to support your colleagues' ability to work collaboratively and engage in team work. The EYPS award is not concerned with the management responsibilities of the setting as this falls outside the remit of the standards for EYPS.

Point for Reflection

Formosinho (2003) likened management to focusing on action hierarchy and rules while leadership is linked to philosophy relationships and influence.

As an EYP, you will need to show how you are able to create and maintain a culture of collaborative and cooperative working with colleagues, both in your own setting and amongst your professional colleagues who may work in one of the many services within the childcare workforce. Chapter 8 will help you to explore the concept of team work and collaboration in more depth.

Being an EYP doesn't mean that you can throw your weight around! You will need to evidence the ways in which you have taken the lead in supporting your colleagues to develop their understanding about effective ways in which they can help babies, toddlers and young children to learn and develop. Try to reflect on the times when you have been involved in influencing and implementing policies and practice and, where appropriate, identify any times when you may have worked collaboratively or taken the lead within a multi-professional team context.

Points for Reflection

Team work and collaboration:

Look at the EYPS standards:

Reflect on your experiences as a leader in this area and identify any sources of evidence that will support you, for example policies that you have contributed to, notes of planning meetings that you have been involved in, planning documents that you have produced.

How do you support your colleagues in your setting or in other settings or in a network to:

- ✓ improve children's well-being, learning and
  development? ⇒ S33
- ✓ plan, deliver, evaluate and improve practice and
  provision?
- ✓ draw on each others' knowledge and skills and to
  share expertise?
- ✓ ensure that everyone has a clear understanding of
  their roles and responsibilities? ⇒ S34
- ✓ ensure that everyone understands the planned objectives
  for each activity and their role in executing them?
- ✓ review and evaluate their practice?
- ✓ assess their current effectiveness and knowledge
  of best practice?
- ✓ continuously review existing policy and practices?
- ✓ influence and shape the policies and practices of
  the setting? ⇒ S35
- ✓ formulate and implement new policies?

(Adapted from CWDC Guidance to the Standards (2008b))

Personal Professional Development

Finally, this area of the standards (S37–39) Personal Professional Development is concerned with the way that you manage your own and your colleagues' professional development needs and the way that you use your ability to be a reflective practitioner. You must demonstrate the ways in which your leadership and support of others encourage a learning culture that will keep both you and your colleagues up to date with current research, new initiatives and early years practices. To gain EYPS you must show your commitment to continuous professional development for both yourself and your colleagues.

Points for Reflection

Claxton (2002) in Rodd (2006) regards the development of dispositions for lifelong learning as fundamental for leaders who are responsible for enabling and evaluating other people. Because effective leaders need to be better learners so that they can help others to learn more effectively, they need to strengthen their own learning power by developing what Claxton refers to as the four Rs of learning power (2002: 17):

- **resilience** (being ready, willing and able to lock on to learning)
- **resourcefulness** (being ready, willing and able to learn in different ways)
- **reflectiveness** (being ready, willing and able to become more strategic about learning) and
- **reciprocity** (being ready, willing and able to learn alone and with others).

As an early years leader, reflect on the bullet points below and identify a time when you supported yourself and others to develop competencies in literacy, numeracy and information and communication technology (ICT) and other professional development needs:

Look at the EYPS standards:

- willing and able to lock on to learning
- able to learn in different ways
- able to be more strategic about learning   ⇒ S37
- able to learn alone   ⇒ S38
- able to learn with others.   ⇒ S39

I often relate the CWDC 39th national standard to John Buchan's 39 steps! There are a lot of standards and the content within each standard is very significant. To begin your EYPS journey, I would advise you reflect on one area of the standards at a time and record your emotional highs and lows. 'Writing down what we are thinking and how we are feeling is a vital part of the reflective process, which is such an important part of adult and professional learning' (National Professional Qualification in Integrated Centre Leadership, p. 26). Keep your reflective log up to date and record any evidence that you may have to support your claim. Your reflective log will act as a record and will support your preparation for the Gateway Review, the Written Tasks and the Setting Visit, as discussed in Chapter 2.

Chapters 9 and 10 will provide you with more information about the requirements of the assessment process and ways in which you can prepare yourself.

Reflective Activity

Personal Professional Development: **Look at the EYPS standards:**

1. Reflect on the ways that you support your colleagues in your setting or in other settings or in a network in this area.
2. Identify any sources of documentary evidence from this area that will support your Setting Visit assessment.

The sources of documentary evidence that you identify must be ones that you have contributed to, for example research briefing notes, planning documents, training needs analysis, etc.

How do you work collaboratively with your colleagues to:

✓ reflect upon and evaluate the effectiveness of their practice? ⇒ S37
✓ modify and adapt their approach where necessary?
✓ draw on research outcomes and other sources of effective practice as a way of informing and improving practice?

How do you:

✓ identify your own additional professional development and support needs? ⇒ S38

> ✓ gain access to sources of continuing professional development and support for yourself and your colleagues?
>
> How do you work collaboratively with your colleagues to:
>
> ✓ review, evaluate and improve practice and provision in order to achieve the best possible outcomes for babies, toddlers and young children?   ⇒ S39
> ✓ encourage innovations in a construcive way?
> ✓ adapt practice if benefits and improvements are perceived?
> ✓ be open about making innovative suggestions?
> ✓ put forward their ideas and adapt their practice?
>
> (Adapted from the CWDC Guidance to the Standards (2008b.))

 Key Points

✓ Identify where you are starting from and plan ahead.
✓ Set yourself some Smart Goals.
✓ Reflect on emotional intelligence.
✓ Reflect, review, analzse and evaluate your experience of leading practice.
✓ Keep your reflective log up to date and record recent examples from your practice to demonstrate the standards.
✓ Be a better learner so that you can help others to learn more effectively.

Further Reading

Bottle, G. (2007) 'The Leadership in the Early Years', in A.D. Nurse, *The New Early Years Professional Early Years*. Oxon: Routledge.

Children's Workforce Development Council (CWDC) (2008) *Guidance to the Standards for the Award of Early Years Professional Status*. London: CWDC.

Jaeckle, S. (2006) 'Early Childhood: A Guide for Students', in T. Bruce, *Managing Yourself and Your Learning*. London: Sage.

Useful Websites

Professor Ferre Laevers – www.ecd.govt.nz/publications/convention/Laevers.pdf
The Early Years Foundation Stage – www.standards.dcsf.gov.uk/eyfs/
The Foundation Stage Forum – www.foundation-stage.info/

CHAPTER 4

WHAT IS EFFECTIVE PRACTICE?

To gain EYPS, your own effective practice with babies, toddlers and young children as well as your leadership and support of others will be assessed. Due to the importance placed on the EYP to deliver 'Effective Practice', the theme will be continued in Chapters 5 to 7.

This chapter now invites you to explore current theory and research findings concerned with the concept of high-quality early years provision. You will be invited to reflect on a number of quality assurance schemes and approaches that have been adopted over the past decade by leaders of effective practice to raise the quality of their provision. The Quality Improvement Principles that underpin the EYFS framework (DCSF, 2008b) will also be examined within the context of the EYP's leadership role. The EYPS National Standards 1–6 will be linked throughout this chapter as they set out the knowledge and understanding that underpins the EYPS Effective Practice standards that you will be expected to meet.

Effective Practice

How do you measure your own effective practice? For an EYP, the notion of effective practice is a double-edged sword – on one hand, you will be expected to engage in effective practice yourself in order to provide positive outcomes for babies, toddlers and young children. On the other hand, you will be expected to model and lead effective practice to your colleagues. As an EYP, you will engage in periods of 'reflective' practice to identify the benefits to your colleagues, the children and families. Research on the topic of effective practice is included in the KEEP (DfES, 2005b) framework (illustrated in Chapter 1) and the EPPE study (Sylva et al., 2004) and its sister project 'Researching Effective Pedagogy in the Early Years' (Siraj-Blatchford et al., 2002). These research projects are well known for the ways in which they have influenced national policies and frameworks, for example the EYPS National Standards (CWDC, 2008b) and the statutory EYFS framework (2008b). Effectiveness research, therefore, can be pivotal in identifying effective practice, which in turn can be used to guide curriculum development, resource deployment, staff ratios, staff qualifications and ways to work with parents (Pugh and Duffy, 2006: 166).

Point for Reflection

'As graduates, the depth and breadth of EYPs' knowledge and understanding enable them to practise and model practice at a high level, and to reflect upon their own practice in order to effect continuous improvement. Their personal practice, and their leadership and support of colleagues, are rooted in a secure grasp of important sources such as national policy, legislation and non-statutory frameworks and guidance, and underlying theories and research on child development and early years practice. Thus informed, EYPs can explain to colleagues and parents the rationale for policy, practice and improvement'. (CWDC, 2008b)

High-quality Provision

EYPs have an important role to play in supporting high-quality provision across all PVI settings. 'Working with the Department for Children, Schools and Families, the National Children's Bureau has set up a national peer support network, the National Quality Improvement Network, made up of representatives drawn from local authorities and national organizations'. The Bureau has also published a set of good practice principles and guidance that link to other quality improvement initiatives that support delivery of the Early Years Foundation Stage (for example, training being developed by the Children's Workforce Development Council) (NCB 2009). Table 4.1 (p. 67) illustrates the national Quality Improvement Network's (NQIN) Quality Improvement Principles.

The NQIN supersedes and replaces the DfES (2002) Investors in Children initiative which endorsed over 48 schemes by 2004. In the past, those of you working across the childcare sector may have become confused by the number and variety of Quality Assurance schemes that were available and ones that you may have adopted may no longer be endorsed by central government today.

EYPS standard 24 asks you to demonstrate your accountability for the delivery of high-quality early years provision. Through your own practice, your graduate studies and your continuous professional development, you will by now have formed a personal view of what constitutes *high-quality provision*.

Reflective Activity

What informs your pedagogy?

Many of the early years pioneers and their successors, for example Professor Ferre Laevers, Maria Montessori, Margaret McMillan, Frederick Froebel and the leaders from Reggio Emillio embrace strong pedagogical beliefs. Their philosophies are based on a strong principled approach and they 'stick to them!' Pedagogy is professional practice relating to the learning and development of babies, toddlers and young children.

1. Who or what informs your pedagogy?
2. What are your principles?
3. How do you convey these to others?
4. Reflect on this and record your thoughts in your reflective log.

Bruce (2006: 69) believes that 'high quality, integrated, early childhood provision, with a strong educational component, can make a difference to children's life chances'. The development of SureStart was established to promote universal access to high quality childcare. As discussed in Chapter 1, the overarching aim of the government's drive to promote high-quality early years provision is for every child to be able to fulfil their potential. In leading high-quality provision, you must be able to show how you meet these challenges and the way in which you acknowledge accountability.

While studying for my Masters Degree in Educational Leadership, I discovered the Japanese philosophical principle of 'Kaizen', a Japanese word meaning continuous improvement. For EYPs to apply this principle, you should keep thinking, 'how can I improve my personal practice and support teams or individuals so that together we can make a difference?'. I believe that as a philosophy, the key to Kaizen for EYPs is in gaining involvement and a commitment to quality improvement which means that everyone should be striving to do everything better every day regardless of their position. In the 1980s, Tom Peters talked about 'living in a nanosecond culture' which relates nicely to the role of the EYP and the way that we have to be responsive to the changes in government direction and policy today.

As leaders of effective early years practice, we can learn from the work of the quality gurus and their theories and interpret their findings to suit our purposes. The work of American leadership gurus who featured in 1950s Japan: for example, Joseph Juran, W. Edwards Deming, and Armand Feigenbum; the Japanese quality gurus who developed and extended the early American quality ideas and models: Kaoru Ishikawa, Genichi Taguchi, and Shigeo Shingo; and the 1970–80s American Western gurus, notably Philip Crosby and Tom Peters was aimed at corporate business – our business is to provide effective early years provision. The quality gurus developed QA tools such as the Plan, Do, Check cycle, the Pareto Analysis, cause and effect diagrams, process control charts, management by walking about (MBWA), the McKinsey 7-S Framework, to name a few. Just because they were developed for industry doesn't mean to say that we can't adopt them to use as early years quality improvement tools.

I particularly like the concept of the Pareto Analysis, which is best described as the 'eighty twenty rule', meaning that if you are not careful, 80 per cent of your time is spent on only 20 per cent of what you are actually accountable for.

 Reflective Activity

Identify who you are accountable to for the delivery of high-quality provision and in what ways.

Reflect on whether your time is spread evenly or not, between:

✓ children (aged 0–5 years)
✓ parents and carers
✓ colleagues
✓ your manager
✓ the governors
✓ your network
✓ the local authority
✓ other professionals.

Look at the EYPS standard:

⇒ S24

The policy focus on quality in the early years has drawn significantly on recent research and in particular the findings of the DfES-funded longitudinal study of Effective Provision of Pre-School Education (EPPE, Sylva et al., 2004 in Bruce, 2006: 3). The research identified the following key indicators of quality early years provision:

✓ highly qualified practitioners
✓ an equal balance of child-initiated and adult-led learning and play activities
✓ adult-child interactions that encourage children to think deeply and express their ides (sustained shared thinking; see EYPS S16)
✓ practitioners with knowledge of how young children learn
✓ practitioners' understanding of the early years curriculum
✓ strong links between the home and the early years setting.

All of the settings in the EPPE project were observed using the revised ECERS–R, the extended ECERS-E and the Caregiver Interaction Scales (CIS) to assess the quality of provision for 3–5-year-old children, and the project found an important link between quality as measured by the scales and children's educational and social development. You may be familiar with the use of ECERS-R (Harms, 2004) and the ITERS-R Environment Rating Scales (Harms et al., 2002). These were both primarily designed to assess the quality of early years provision. You may have used ITERS-R as a rating scale to assess the quality of provision for children from birth to 30 months or the ECERS-R, which is designed for children under 30 months to five years and which describes the characteristics of the physical environment and the quality of the children's social and pedagogical environment. The ECERS-R rating scale describes 43 areas under the following seven areas:

- space and furnishings
- personal care routines
- language reasoning
- activities
- interactions
- programme structure
- parents and staff.

Each area is rated on a seven-point scale (1 = inadequate, 3 = minimal/adequate and 5 = good with 7 being excellent). One authority believes that 'The fact that the Environment Rating Scales and the aspects of quality they measure are so predictive of children's development makes them valuable tools not only for assessing, but also for improving the quality of early years provision' (Advisory Service Kent (www.kenttrustweb.org.uk/ask), 2008). However, your graduate studies will have informed you to be cautious in interpreting such research studies – you may wish to consider a number of reasons that would lead to a link between the quality of provision and the development of children.

Case Study of an ITERS-R Audit Undertaken by a Local Authority Advisor/EYPS Candidate who achieved the status

Context:

I observed what the staff did when they took the babies outside, and linked them to my widespread reading around the six areas of learning in the EYFS (Early Years Foundation Stage). These focus on providing more sensory experiences and developing the babies' acquisition of language skills. The EYFS says that staff should aim to take children outside at least once a day.

I administered the ITERS over a number of days and where appropriate in discussion with the room leaders, to ensure that I could fully understand and assess the setting's environment and the babies' needs. Using ITERS was effective as it enabled me to assess the quality of the provision.

When I fed back the findings of the ITERS audit, I was very happy with the initial comments and actions taken by the practitioners to the suggestions/improvements that I had recommended. These included:

- providing a sheltered place to lay a rug on the grass for babies to be placed upon
- giving babies the opportunity to crawl into sand pits and water
- letting babies explore the indoor and outdoor environment
- singing with the babies outdoors and indoors
- providing resources for babies to grasp, to pull themselves up onto and for low level climbing to occur
- providing objects outdoors that are 'bigger' than those provided inside
- allowing babies to take 'safe risks'
- selecting books for the book area and monitoring their use as babies at this age range do have a tendency to 'mouth' the corners! Soft material, hardbacked books are best and staff need to be prepared to throw them out and buy new ones.

There was an improvement to the interactions and communications with babies. Over time I witnessed that, for example, I noticed that some of the practitioners began rolling the ball to some of the babies and were commenting on the sounds that objects being tapped together make. I left highlighted photocopies of what needs to be actioned to achieve excellence all round so that the practitioners and room leaders can use these as a self-evaluation/development tool.

In reviewing the ECERS-E system, Papatheodorou (2004) suggested that it does not provide a clear description of what constitutes 'quality in the early years'. 'Implicitly, the subscales and the corresponding items are seen as the defining indicators of quality. However, as the ECERS-E is a scale that looks at quality in terms of academic achievement, it is important that the early years practitioners do not rely on this scale alone' (2004). For EYPs, then, to promote the underlying philosophy of early years provision which is to support babies, toddlers and young children's holistic development, you may want to consider combining ECERS-E and ECERS-R to gain a richer picture of the quality in your early years setting.

Reflective Activity

'In Britain, researchers and practitioners in the early years and childcare field are arguing that quality improvement processes are important for the following reasons' (NQIN, 2008):	Record the answers to these questions in your EYPS reflective log:
All young children, in whatever setting, deserve the highest quality care that we can provide for them.	How do you ensure high quality provision?
Parents choosing and then engaging with early years providers should have a recognized way of knowing that those settings are taking part in continuous quality improvement.	What quality improvement systems do you use?
Research shows us that quality is a continuous process: a journey rather than a destination, and that providers need to be involved in self-reflection and peer support as part of the everyday life of their settings.	How do you engage in self-reflection peer support?
Research also shows us that, in order to be effective, this process needs some form of regular external verification.	Who do you work in partnership with to externally QA your setting?
Both research and the experience of local authority and voluntary sector advisors have shown that systematic, workplace-based	Identify ways that you have worked collaboratively to bring about quality improvements.

(Continued)

(Continued)

quality improvement processes are
the single most effective means of raising
the quality of settings for young children.

Ofsted inspections, while a vital part of the
quality improvement process, cover only the
minimum national standards, only take place.
over one day, once every three years, and put
settings in one of only four broad categories
of quality.

How have you used Ofsted
inspections to improve and
sustain quality?

Systematic quality improvement processes
offer local authorities a way of supporting and
monitoring quality within their settings – this
will become even more important as they plan
to meet the duty to provide sufficient childcare
for their areas and as they consider ways of
integrating children's services.

Identify the type and range of
quality improvement processes
that you have been involved in.

Systematic quality improvement also acts as a
research tool and a method of gathering data
about improvements in quality
over time and about those areas
of practice which need additional support and
training.

Identify an area of
practice that you
have gathered data on over a
period of time and have used to
access additional support and
training.

Look at the EYPS standards:
⇒ S6, S24, S36

This activity was devised using information from the National Children's Bureau
website: http://ncb.org.uk/page.asp?txt//origin × 341 cz

In claiming EYPS S24, you may wish to consider The National Quality Improvement Network Research Team Quality Improvement Principles (NQIN, 2007 as illustrated in Table 4.1). As discussed of previously 'Quality improvement leaders in national organizations and local authorities have come together under the National Children's Bureau (NCB) umbrella to create a National Quality Improvement Network (NQIN) to keep quality improvement high on the agenda' (NQIN, 2007: 5). The network was funded by the Department for Education and Skills (DfES) to produce a set of good practice principles for quality improvement processes/quality assurance schemes for a whole-setting approach, as illustrated in Table 4.1. The NQIN (2008) have produced a companion guide to illustrate the Quality Improvement Priniciples illustrated in Table 4.1.

Table 4.1 *The NQIN five themes and corresponding National Quality Improvement Principles (NQIN, 2008)*

Theme 1: Early years and chilcare settings improve outcomes
Principle 1: Guide and support settings to improve outcomes.

Theme 2: Values and principles are inclusive and address inequality
Principle 2: Encourage settings to be inclusive and reduce inequalities.
Principle 3: Strengthen values and principles in settings.

Theme 3: Continuous self-evalution and reflective practice
Principle 4: Promote effective practice and its delivery in settings.
Principle 5: Increase the capacity of settings to improve quality.
Principle 9: Support settings through the self-evaluation and improvement processes.

Theme 4: Effective leadership and workforce planning
Principle 6: Promote integrated working within and among settings.
Principle 7: Challenge and support key people in settings to lead quality improvement.
Principle 8: Build on settings' proven workforce development strategies.

Theme 5: Effective monitoring snd evalition of practice and outcomes
Principle 10: Local authorities and national organizations monitor quality improvements and communicate achievements.
Principle 11: Local authorities and national organizations ensure quality improvement is achievable, continuous and sustainable.
Principle 12: Schemes operate fair, inclusive and transparent accreditation processes.

The continuous improvement approch based on the Quality Improvement Themes and Principles is not about ticking boxes, but about enabling children's trusts, local authorities and settings to develop and deliver their vision for better outcomes for children and families.

Source: National Quality Improvement Network (2008).

Effective Practice and the Early Years Foundation Stage (DCSF, 2008d)

One of your biggest challenges was more likely than not how you led the implementation of the statutory EYFS framework (DCSF, 2008d). Your interpretation of the accountabilities and responsibilities set out in the *Practice Guidance for the Early Years Foundation Stage* (DCSF, 2008a) will have informed your own practice and the way that you supported others through the transition.

As the EYFS framework is based on a principled approach, your EYPS assessments will need to show that you understand the EYFS four guiding themes and their associated four underlying broad principles, which are illustrated in Table 4.2. Equally important is the way that you use this information to inform your own practice, your leadership and

Table 4.2   *EYFS themes*

EYFS Theme 1: A Unique Child	**EYFS Theme 2: Positive Relationships**
Every child is a competent learner from birth who can be resilient, capable, confident and self-assured (DCSF, 2008)	Children learn to be strong and independent from a base of loving and secure relationships with parents and/or a key person (DCSF, 2008)
Underlying Principles:	**Underlying Principles:**
1.1 Child development	2.1 Respecting each other
1.2 Inclusive practice	2.2 Parents as partners
1.3 Keeping safe	2.3 Supporting learning
1.4 Health and well-being	2.4 Key person
EYFS Theme 3: Enabling Environments	**EYFS Theme 4: Learning and Development**
The environment plays a key role in supporting and extending children's development and learning (DCSF, 2008)	Children develop and learn in different ways and at different rates and all areas of Learning and Development are equally important and inter-connected (DCSF, 2008)
Underlying Principles:	**Underlying Principles:**
3.1 Observation and assessment	4.1 Play and exploration
3.2 Supporting every child	4.2 Active learning
3.3 The learning environment	4.3 Creativity and critical thinking
3.4 The wider context	4.4 Areas of learning and development

the ways in which you support others to interpret them. While the EYFS framework provides a systematic and structured approach to early years provision, it does not provide guidance on ways to develop the necessary leadership and management competencies that are required to ensure its successful implementation (Chapter 9 will therefore explore ways of leading effective early years systems, processes and people).

The EYFS set the scene for EYPs to play a significant role in becoming the British government's inspirational early years change agents. Your EYPS assessments will need to show how you personally practice, model and led your colleagues through the changes to design, implement and deliver effective early years provision in your setting, network or service. To explain your commitment to the five Every Child Matters (DfES:2003b) outcomes of staying safe, being healthy, enjoying and achieving, making a positive contribution and achieving economic well-being consider how you lead and promoted:

- high standards
- provision of equality of opportunity and inclusive practices
- working-in-partnership with parents, carers and other professionals
- continuous Quality Improvement
- laying of secure foundations for children's future life and learning.

Reflective Activity

Identify:

1. How do you promote the EYFS four guiding themes and each set of accompanying four broad principles within your setting, placement or network?
2. Consider how your own effective practice and the ways that you lead and support others promotes:

- the delivery of effective practice
- an understanding about current research findings
- ways of providing developmentally appropriate resources.

Look at the EYPS standards:

⇒ S1, S9, S10, S11, S12, S14, S21

Leading the EYFS Areas of Learning and Development

For the purpose of your Gateway Review, your Written Tasks and your Setting Visit, you will need to explain the ways in which you practice, model and lead the EYFS areas of learning and development to your assessor. To do this, you may want to reflect on the 'Leadership point of view' activity that you undertook in Chapter 2 and the 'What informs your pedagogy?' reflective activity featured earlier in this chapter.

The aim of these activities is to help you explain to others how you lead effective practice. To be an effective EYP, it is important that you are clear about your thoughts on the way that you lead. This will not only help your colleagues but also help your assessor understand where you are coming from and will also help to clarify what you expect of others and what they can expect from you. The EYFS is made up of six areas of learning and development:

- Personal, Social and Emotional Development (PSED)
- Communication, Language and Literacy (CLL)
- Problem Solving, Reasoning and Numeracy (PSRN)
- Knowledge and Understanding of the World (KUW)
- Physical Development (PD)
- Creative Development (CD)

Remember that these areas are all equally important, connected and underpinned by the principles of the EYFS illustrated in Table 4.2 which you will need to show understanding of for EYPS S1. As an EYP, your knowledge and understanding of the six overlapping stages of child development (illustrated in Table 4.3) in the EYFS will also need to be demonstrated in your assessments.

Remember that while you need to show accountability for high-quality provision in the EYFS, you will also need to show your understanding of the ways that the EYFS statutory Welfare Requirements (DCSF, 2008b) interconnect. These are:

- safeguarding and promoting children's welfare
- a suitable person
- suitable premises, environment and equipment
- organization.

These will all be explored further in Chapter 6.

Table 4.3   *EYFS Child development overview (DCSF, 2007c)*

Birth–11 months

During this period, young children's physical development is very rapid and they gain increasing control of their muscles. They also develop skills in moving their hands, feet, limbs and head, quickly becoming mobile and able to handle and manipulate objects. They are learning from the moment of birth. Even before their first words, they find out a lot about language by hearing people talking, and are especially interested when it involves themselves and their daily lives. Sensitive caregiving, which responds to children's growing understanding and emotional needs, helps to build secure attachments to special people such as parents, family members or carers. Regular, though flexible, routines help young children to gain a sense of order in the world and to anticipate events. A wide variety of experience, which involves all the senses, encourages learning and an interest in the environment.

8–20 months

As children become mobile, new opportunities for exploration and exercise open up. A safe and interesting environment, with age-appropriate resources, helps children to develop curiosity, coordination and physical abilities. This is a time when children can start to learn the beginnings of self-control and how to relate to other people. In this period, children can be encouraged to develop their social and mental skills by people to whom they have a positive attachment. Building on their communication skills, children now begin to develop a sense of self and are more able to express their needs and feelings. Alongside non-verbal communication, children learn a few simple words for everyday things and people. With encouragement and plenty of interaction with carers, children's communication skills grow and their vocabulary expands very rapidly during this period.

16–26 months

Children in this phase are usually full of energy and need careful support to use it well. Growing physical strengths and skills mean that children need active times for exercise, and quiet times for calmer activities. Playing with other children is an important new area for learning. This helps children to better understand other people's thoughts and feelings, and to learn how to cooperate with others. Exploration and simple self-help builds a sense of self-confidence. Children are also learning about boundaries and how to handle frustration. Play with toys that come apart and fit together encourages problem solving and simple planning. Pretend play helps children to learn about a range of possibilities. Adults are an important source of security and comfort.

Table 4.3   (Continued)

22–36 months

Children's fine motor skills continue to develop and they enjoy making marks, using a variety of materials, looking at picture books and listening to stories, important steps in literacy. Self-help and independence soon emerge if adults support and encourage children in areas such as eating, dressing and toileting. Praise for new achievements helps to build their self-esteem. In this phase, children's language is developing rapidly and many are beginning to put sentences together. Joining in conversations with children is an important way for children to learn new things and to begin to think about past, present and future. Developing physical skills mean that children can now usually walk, climb and run, and join in active play with other children. This is an important time for learning about dangers and safe limits.

30–50 months

An increased interest in joint play such as make-believe, construction and games helps children to learn the important social skills of sharing and cooperating. Children also learn more about helping adults in everyday activities and finding a balance between independence and complying with the wishes of others. Children still need the comfort and security of special people. Close, warm relationships with carers form the basis for much learning, such as encouraging children to make healthy choices in food and exercise. At this stage, children are becoming more aware of their place in a community. Literacy and numeracy can develop rapidly with the support of a wide range of interesting materials and activities. Children's language is now much more complex, as many become adept at using longer sentences. Conversations with adults become a more important source of information, guidance and reassurance.

40–60+ months

During this period, children are now building a stronger sense of their own identity and their place in a wider world. Children are learning to recognize the importance of social rules and customs, to show understanding and tolerance of others, and to learn how to be more controlled in their own behaviour. Learning and playing in small groups help to foster the development of social skills. Children now become better able to plan and undertake more challenging activities with a wider range of materials for making and doing. In this phase, children learn effectively in shared activities with more able peers and adults. Literacy and problem solving, reasoning and numeracy skills continue to develop. Children's developing understanding of cause and effect is encouraged by the introduction of a wider variety of equipment, media and technologies.

What Can Leaders Learn from Other Approaches?

Reggio Emilia

Throughout my career as a teacher, lecturer and Head of School in early years, I have always been receptive to the influences of alternative education systems and what we can glean from them to improve our own practice. You may have come across the Reggio Emilia approach, whereby young children are encouraged to explore their understanding of their experiences through different media, for example words, gestures, discussion, mime, movement, drawing, painting, constructions, sculpture, shadow play, mirror play, drama and music.

An EYP modelling ways to involve the child in child-initiated play

High levels of expression are reached by Reggio Emilian children in many forms of symbolic representation, particularly the graphic arts, which in turn are documented by the pedagogical staff and the children themselves. Small groups of children work together – often with an adult – all around the educational setting, which has been organised so as to facilitate social, cognitive, verbal and symbolic constructions. (Directorate for Education, 2004)

The EYP's role within the Reggio Emilia approach would involve working as co-practitioner as the role of the practitioner is fundamentally to be that of a 'learner' alongside the child. In the Reggio approach, you become a practitioner-researcher, a resource and guide offering your experience to the children. Within Reggio Emilia settings, the practitioners are committed to reflection about their own teaching and learning and great attention is given to the look and feel of the classroom. The environment is considered to be the 'third teacher'.

    Point for Reflection

'The enduring nature of the Reggio Emilia schools can be explained partially by the inspired leadership of its late founder, Loris Malaguzzi, and the high level of quality sustained in the early childhood centres by their dedicated staff' (Directorate for Education, 2004)

Professor Ferre Laevers

While working as a LA advisory teacher, I was privileged to be introduced to the Experiential Education (EXE) model founded by Professor Ferre Laevers which I used to support early years practitioners in improving the quality of their work. His theory is based on a 'process-oriented approach' and supports a belief that the most convincing way to assess the quality of any educational setting is to focus on the degree of 'emotional well-being' and the level of 'involvement' of the children.

As an EYP, you will of course be concerned with ensuring the best possible outcomes for children to develop and learn, and to do this, you will actively involve others in using such processes. The EXE model encourages you to look at the child and their experience of the care and learning environment. It can help you to become aware of the strengths and weaknesses in your provision through:

- assessment of the actual levels of well-being and involvement of the babies, toddlers and young children
- the analysis of observations undertaken
- the selection and implementation of actions to improve quality.

Points for Reflection

Consider Ferre Laevers' concept of the 'process within the child'

To gain insight into the practice in your early years setting, service or network, answer these questions:

✓ Is the space arranged to promote babies, toddlers and young children's gross and fine motor development?

✓ What resources are on offer, for each age range, and do they promote language development?

✓ What and how many activities are on offer for each age range and do they promote curiosity?

✓ How are practitioners relating to children?

✓ Are the children relating to one another?

✓ How is the room organized, and does it promote opportunities for children to become independent?

✓ Is everything safe, and are there opportunities for children to develop self-confidence?

✓ How much guidance have you given to other practitioners or to the children.

Look at the EYPS standards:

⇒ S6, S8, S10, S12

The EXE model can be used to assess the impact of the environment on children's play. While leading effective practice, you may proactively review and change the environment as a result of observing children's well-being and involvement. Some of the settings that I supported transformed their practice from a practitioner-oriented to a child-oriented way of arranging things.

The official Ofsted inspection for the LA that I worked in noted the improvement. 'Staff have re-arranged the nursery and resources to support children's learning, allow them to use their initiative and select freely and independently from a wide selection of purposeful and meaningful activities appropriate to their individual needs' (Colleen Marin's presentation, at the 2nd OECD 'Starting Strong Network' workshop in 2007).

Te Whāriki

The Te Whāriki system is based on children's uniqueness as learners, their ethnicity and their rights in New Zealand society. It is based on contemporary theory and research related to young children's psychology and learning. It supports the Maori principle of 'empowering children to learn and grow' and has five significant themes:

- Mana Atua – well-being
- Mana Whenua – belonging
- Mana Tangata – contribution
- Mana Reo – communication
- Mana Aoturoa – exploration

    Point for Reflection

A woven mat for all to stand on
'The title of the curriculum, Te Whāriki, is a central metaphor. Firstly, the early childhood curriculum is envisaged as a Whāriki, a woven mat 'for all to stand on'... Secondly, the metaphor describes a 'spider web' model of curriculum for children, in contrast to a step model' (Carr and May, 2000 in Penn, 2000).

Leading the effective delivery of Te Whāriki is based on:

- the arrangements of the physical environment and equipment
- the scheduling of activities and events
- the organizational philosophies, policies and procedures
- the inclusion and support of parents and the connections with the community
- the ages of the children, group size and groupings.

A child developing pre-writing skills in an EYP's setting

The High/Scope Approach

The early years High/Scope approach supports a set of principles that EYPs may decide to follow. The principles of the High/Scope approach are intended to be used as an 'open framework' that can be adapted to the specific needs of the provision. The principles are based on a belief that children (aged 0–5 years) learn best through active experiences with people, materials, events and ideas, rather than through direct adult-initiated and structured activities. EYPs leading High/Scope practice will promote a belief to others that children learn best while pursuing their personal interests and goals and that they should be encouraged to make choices about materials and activities throughout the day. I once observed pre-school children engaging in the High/Scope system of 'plan, do and review'. The practitioner-leader provided the children with big books illustrating activities for them to make choices from at the start of the session, they then planned what to do and set up their activities. The children explored their activities while asking and answering questions, solving problems and interacting with their peers and other practitioners.

It is very important that the values and principles that underpin the EYP's own effective practice and leadership of others are based on research, evidence and trustworthy theories. As discussed in this chapter, much of what is deemed to be effective practice is readily available in national guidance from government departments, for example the DCSF, 2008a, *Practice Guidance,* highlights the importance of Quality

Improvement and using self-evaluation to drive Ofsted inspection. As an EYP, you will have formed your own opinions about effective practice based on your own research and critical analysis of theories, government documents, frameworks and guidance, and you will naturally draw on and complement what is on offer.

 Key Points

As a leader of effective early years practice:

✓ Create a commitment towards quality improvement in the EYFS (S1).
✓ Adopt a new philosophy: 'KAIZEN – everyone should be striving for continuous improvement regardless of their position' (S33).
✓ Embrace a strong vision and a strong pedagogical belief and promote these to others.
✓ Identify areas for improvement, as leaders are accountable for high-quality provision (S24).
✓ Keep your self up to date with research findings and effective early years practices (S38).
✓ Introduce contemporary methods of working based on your research evidence (S39).
✓ Harness everyone's potential so that they are working together effectively (S38).
✓ Eliminate practices that are prescriptive and those that do not promote positive outcomes for children (S39).
✓ Establish a dynamic programme of continuous professional development (S38).

Further Reading

DfES (2002) *Researching Effective Pedagogy in the Early Years*. DfES: Norwich.

Directorate for Education (2004) *Starting Strong Curricula and Pedagogies in Early Childhood Education and Care: Five Curriculum Outlines*. OECD: Stockholm.

Laevers, F. (ed.) (1994) *Defining and Assessing Quality in Early Childhood Education*. Belgium: Laevers University Press.

National Quality Improvement Network (2008) *Companion Guide to the Quality Improvement Principles*. London: National Children's Bureau.

Pascal, C. and Bertram, T. (1997) *Effective Early Learning. Case Studies on Improvement*. London: Sage.

Useful Websites

Early Childhood Environment Rating Scales – www.fpg.unc.edu/~ecers/
Early Years Foundation Stage – www.standards.dfes.gov.uk/eyfs/
High/Scope – www.highscope.org

CHAPTER 5

EARLY YEARS EFFECTIVE PRACTICE – ASSESSMENT ARRANGEMENTS, ROUTINES AND COMMUNICATION, LANGUAGE AND LITERACY

This chapter will explore the EYP role related to leading effective assessment arrangements, baby, toddler and young children's routines and ways of leading and supporting effective early communication, language and literacy development. The chapter will examine the statutory and non-statutory requirements that are used to inform effective assessment arrangements within the early years context (S9, S11). Leading effective practice for children's (0–5) early years communication, language and literacy skills will be explored within the perspective of what is developmentally appropriate for the early years (S22, S15 and S16). As with the previous chapter (Chapter 4), this chapter will encourage you to reflect on the depth and breadth of your knowledge and understanding against the specified content of each standard and help you to consider how this knowledge and understanding informs:

- your own personal reflective practice
- the way that you model behaviours and best practice to others
- your leadership and support of effective practice to others.

As the EYPS National Standards 1–6 are concerned with your personal practice, your relationships with children, your collaboration with parents and colleagues, and your own professional development, they will be linked throughout this chapter.

Effective Early Years Assessments

The Statutory Framework for the EYFS (2008b, p. 10) states that practitioners should undertake 'ongoing observational assessment to inform planning for each child's continuing development through play based activities'. This implies that EYPs will use their knowledge and understanding about the most effective way to undertake child observations and use these to plan for the next steps in children's learning and development which will ultimately bring about improved outcomes for the children in their care.

Taylor and Woods (1998) suggest that: 'With the insight from the observations and their assessments, we are better equipped to:

- devise optimum environments to promote the holistic development of each child and respond to his or her needs
- take appropriate action if any aspect of a child's development, behaviour, health or well-being causes us concern and does not appear to be within the range typical for his or her age
- interact more sensitively with children and form happy relationships with them
- monitor, evaluate and improve the provision we make for children, i.e. the care we give, the curriculum we devise and the outcomes we achieve.' (1998)

The EYP standard number 10 asks EYPs to: 'use close informed observations and other strategies to monitor children's activity, development and progress systematically and carefully, and use this information to inform, plan and improve practice and provision' (CWDC, 2008b, p. 61).

To do this, you will need to show how your knowledge and understanding about the most appropriate ways to organize and undertake observational assessments informs your own practice and your ability to create effective systems that are understood by everyone else. This is especially important as child observations are used to inform the planning process and improve practice and provision for individual babies, toddlers and young children's:

- achievement, interests and stages of development
- appropriate play and learning experiences
- expectations of the early learning goals.

The cyclic nature of leading child observation and assessment in order to bring about improved outcomes for children is illustrated in Figure 5.1.

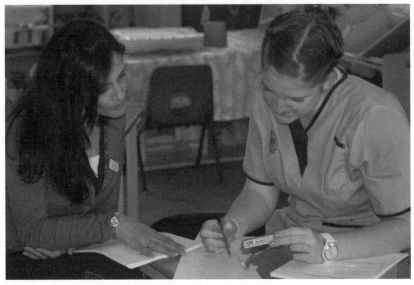

An EYP supporting a practitioner to use ICT to record child observations

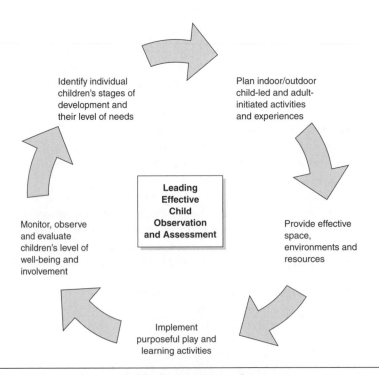

Identify individual
children's stages of
development and
their level of needs

Plan indoor/outdoor
child-led and adult-
initiated activities
and experiences

**Leading
Effective
Child
Observation
and Assessment**

Monitor, observe
and evaluate
children's level of
well-being and
involvement

Provide effective
space,
environments and
resources

Implement
purposeful play and
learning activities

Figure 5.1   *Leading Effective Child Observation and Assessment*

Early Years Foundation Stage Assessment Requirements

The REPEY research suggests that 'the more knowledge the adult has of the child, the better matched their support and the more effective the subsequent learning' (Siraj-Blatchford et al., 2002: 48). EYPs must therefore lead a process of systematic assessment of babies, toddlers and young children in order to meet the assessment and reporting requirements of the EYFS.

The assessment requirements for the EYFS profile (illustrated in Table 5.1) are set out in the Statutory Framework for the EYFS (DCSF: 2008, 16, 17).

Table 5.1   *The EYFS assessment requirements*

Assessment during the EYFS

Ongoing assessment is an integral part of the learning and development process. Providers must ensure that practitioners are observing children and responding appropriately to help them make progress from birth towards the early learning goals. Where practitioners require additional training in order to assess capably and objectively, it is the responsibility of the provider to ensure practitioners receive the support that they need. Assessments should be based on practitioners' observation of what children are doing in their day-to-day activities. As judgements are based on observational evidence gathered from a wide range of learning and teaching contexts, it is expected that all adults who interact with the child should contribute to the process, and that account will be taken of information provided by parents. An essential feature of parental involvement is an ongoing dialogue, building on the partnership begun by any previous practitioner(s). Settings should report progress and achievements to parents throughout the EYFS.

The *Practice Guidance for the Early Years Foundation Stage* sets out detailed formative assessment suggestions in the 'Look, listen and note' sections of the areas of Learning and Development. Practitioners should:

- make systematic observations and assessments of each child's achievements, interests and learning styles
- use these observations and assessments to identify learning priorities and plan relevant and motivating learning experiences for each child
- match their observations to the expectations of the early learning goals.

Assessment at the end of the EYFS – the Early Years Foundation Stage profile

The EYFS Profile is a way of summing up each child's development and learning achievements at the end of the EYFS. It is based on practitioners' ongoing observation and assessments in all six areas of Learning and Development. Each child's level of development must be recorded against the 13 assessment scales derived from the early learning goals. Judgements against these scales, which are set out in Appendix 1 of the *Statutory Framework for the Early Years Foundation Stage*, should be made from observation of consistent and independent behaviour, predominantly children's self-initiated activities.

Some children will have experienced a range of settings during the final year of the EYFS and may have a number of carers. In these cases, the EYFS Profile must be completed by the provider where the child spends the majority of time between 8 am and 6 pm. Providers should take account of all available records and of any formal or informal discussions with the parents and with those involved with children in the previous year.

Children with special educational needs may be working below the level of the scales and require an alternative approach to assessment. In these cases, providers may use the assessment systems of their local authority or other systems according to the needs of the children.

At the end of the EYFS, providers must ensure that children are assessed against the 13 scales in the EYFS Profile. Providers may use the e-Profile (available from local authorities) or their own record-keeping systems. Regulations made under Section 99 of the Childcare Act 2006 require early years providers to provide information about the assessments they carry out to local authorities. Local authorities are under a duty to return this data to the DCSF.

Local authorities have a duty to monitor and moderate the EYFS Profile judgements to ensure that providers are making assessments that are consistent across settings. Providers must take part in these arrangements.

Source: www.standards.dfes.gov.uk/eyfs/site/requirements/learning/assessment.htm

Reflective Activity

Describe the ways in which you support child observations in your Local Authority, setting or network:

1. Is there a time when it has been necessary to observe babies, toddlers or young children either individually or in small groups?
2. How do you encourage others to record observations, for example a written record, a tick chart, a time sample?
3. Do you take account of children's voices or drawings, photographs, digital images, videos or audio recordings?
4. How do you keep records of child observations and for what purpose?
5. How do you discuss child observations with:

   a. children?
   b. colleagues?
   c. key workers?
   d. parents?

6. How do you use child observations as a basis for making differentiated and personalized provision in respect to individual children?
7. How do you plan for children's next steps in the light of their current stage of learning and development?
8. How do you use the child observations to inform individual children's EYFS profiles?
9. How do you seek and use observations of their own children from parents/carers?

Look at the EYPS standards:

⇒ S4, S10

Common Assessment Framework (CAF)

Another significant feature of your role as an EYP is to show how you use your knowledge and understanding of the Common Assessment Framework (CAF) (CWDC, 2007b). The green paper, *Every Child Matters* (DfES, 2003b), proposed the introduction of a national Common Assessment Framework (CAF) as a key part of the strategy for helping children and young people to achieve the paper's five priority outcomes for children and young people of: being healthy, staying safe, enjoying and achieving, making a positive contribution, and achieving economic well-being.

Point for Reflection

Section 10 of the Children Act 2004 places a duty on local authorities and their partners to cooperate to improve the well-being of children and young people, defined by reference to the five ECM outcomes (CWDC, 2008b).

As an EYP, you should show how you are conversant with the role of the lead professional and the aims of the CAF 'to make it easier for agencies to work together and to improve the consistency and quality of assessments, by introducing a common method of assessing the needs of children and young people that could be used by the entire children's workforce' (*Every Child Matters*, 2003b).

The multi-agency approach (S33) to working that underpins the CAF will need to be reflected in your EYPS assessments. You should aim to discuss how you work with professionals in relation to the CAF and provide examples of the ways that you have supported the early identification of individual babies, toddlers and young children's needs. You may also consider explaining how you brief your colleagues about the key objectives of the CAF and how they have managed any cultural changes to implement the CAF.

My research into educational leadership introduced me to the concept of Early Years Leaders being 'orchestrators of change'. Change is a big topic and currently endemic in the early years sector. To show how you lead change effectively, you may wish to consider the factors illustrated in Table 5.2 below:

✓ analyse the changes to be implemented
✓ identify any resistance and barriers to the change
✓ plan innovative strategies
✓ communicate the changes clearly
✓ consult, listen to and respect the viewpoints of others
✓ take things slowly (one step at a time)
✓ eliminate stress levels on any colleagues that may be affected by the change.

Table 5.2 illustrates the success factors for introducing the role of the Lead Professional.

The lead professional is a key element of integrated support. They take the lead to coordinate provision and act as a single point of contact for a child and their family when a range of services are involved and an integrated response is required. (DfES, Every Child Matters, 2003b)

Table 5.2   *The leading professional success factors*

Success factors and barriers to implementation

Success factors	Barriers
1. Enthusiasm at grass roots and managerial level	1. Lack of joining-up across services; conflicts of interest
2. 'Champions' and leaders at all levels	2. Mismatch between the 'vision' and the practice
3. Clear perception of the benefits for children and families	3. Confusion and muddle about processes
4. Participation of children, young people and families	4. Anxiety about increased workload
5. History and practice of multi-agency working	5. Skill/confidence gaps
6. Learning from others	6. Lack of local support
7. Clear structures and processes	
8. Good support for practitioners	

Source: CWDC (2007a)

Reflective Activity

Review any CAF training that you have received from your local authority or your training provider.

- How have you cascaded this to others?
- How have you applied your knowledge about ways to:

    - Use child observations to ensure that important needs are not overlooked?
    - Provide a common structure to record information?
    - Provide information sharing between your colleagues and other agencies?
    - Work with other agencies, to reduce avoidable referrals and enable specialist services to focus their resources where they are most needed?

Look at the EYPS standards:

⇒ S10, S21, 23

Information about the CAF and supporting tools documents can be accessed on the Every Child Matters website: www.everychildmatters.gov. uk/resources-and-practice/ IG00146

Effective Child-centred Activities and Routines (S9, S11)

As with many of the EYP's accountabilities, they are highly complex and at the same time, they can be very multifaceted. The skills that you require to practise, model and promote effective ways to design, plan and facilitate effective daily and weekly routines will draw on your knowledge and understanding about children's (aged 0–5 years) well-being, involvement and developmental needs and interests. You are challenged by not only meeting the children's needs, but also, you need to plan around the daily schedule and, at the same time, meet the needs of your colleagues, parents and carers who may want to influence when the child should eat, sleep or play. As an EYP, you need to consider how you balance all this flexibly. One of my EYPS mentees undertook work experience in a baby unit and was faced with the dilemma of respecting the wishes of three parents all wanting different feeding and sleeping patterns for their babies. The candidate felt challenged by the fact that the babies did not always respond to the routine set by the parents and that the babies never had the opportunity to play together, share mealtimes or go outside at the same time. The candidate resolved the situation by liaising with the setting manager and the parents to come to a mutual understanding about the need to be flexible in order to meet the babies' emotional, social and health and well-being needs.

 Reflective Activity

Identify any routines that you have influenced in your setting, for example:

- ✓ indoor/outdoor play routines
- ✓ meals, snacks and drinks routines
- ✓ personal care routines, for example toileting, hand washing, brushing teeth
- ✓ sleep, rest and relaxation routines
- ✓ routines for children who attend for long periods of time
- ✓ routines for children who attend part time
- ✓ children who attend more than one setting
- ✓ potty training routines
- ✓ routines for children with specified medical conditions
- ✓ routines for children with special educational needs and/or disabilities
- ✓ routines that allow children time to become engrossed in their play activities
- ✓ routines that foster children's independence
- ✓ routines that promote children's personal and social development.

Look at the EYPS standards:

⇒ S9, S11

Wherever possible, you should show how you have designed, planned and implemented effective indoor and outdoor play and learning activities suited to children's (aged 0–5 years) learning and development needs. Access to an outdoor play area is expected to be the norm for providers. In provision where outdoor play space cannot be provided, outings should be planned and taken on a daily basis (unless circumstances make this inappropriate, for example unsafe weather conditions (DCSF, 2008c)).

Point to Remember

Outdoor provision can easily lend itself to supporting young children's natural means of learning. Sensory experience is readily available. Children can observe mini beasts in their natural environment, match leaves of different colours, feel textures and listen to the sound of feet crunching on dry leaves (Dowling in Bruce, 2006: 48).

How do you influence children's (aged 0–5 years) outdoor play?

Look at the EYPS standard:

⇒ S1
⇒ S11

Personalized Provision

In demonstrating how you make personalized provision for children, you will need to show how you lead, model and promote ways to respect and value them, irrespective of their current stage of development or attainment, age, gender, social background, race or ethnicity, learning difficulties and/or disabilities. The EYPS National Standard S7 is concerned with the way that you show your commitment to raising the achievement of all children. The EYPS National Standard S14 asks you to show how you practice, lead and model ways that identify the next steps for individual children's (aged 0–5 years) learning and development, and how this informs your ability to make suitable provision to support effective practice. Factors that will support your explanation about the ways you make personalized provision for all children (aged 0–5 years) are cyclic, as illustrated in Table 5.1.

An EYP candidate modelling a play activity to support the developmental needs of babies

Point to Remember

Providers must plan and organize their systems to ensure that every child receives an enjoyable and challenging learning and development experience that is tailored to meet their individual needs (Statutory Framework for the EYFS, 2008).

The EYPS National Standard 2 sets out the knowledge and understanding that is concerned with how children develop and learn, through your graduate-level studies. Your EYPS assessments must reflect this understanding and the ways in which it informs your personal practice, and the way that you lead your colleagues to plan experiences and activities that are personalized as far as possible to suit the needs and interests of individual children (aged 0–5 years). In doing this, you will of course need to show in your assessments how you take account of the range of children's (aged 0–5 years) physical, cognitive, emotional and social development (see Table 4.3) that is found, during the Foundation Stage, among children of the same chronological age.

You will need to show how your planning systems promote a flexible approach and accommodate the needs of all children (aged 0–5 years) by making provision for their steps in learning and development (Figure 5.1). Of course, your plans will be informed by your observational assessments and will take an inclusive approach (as discussed previously in this chapter). They will also need to show that they are flexible enough to cater for children's different stages of development, for example you may have differentiated learning and play activities or resources to meet the needs of an individual child or a group of children. Another example could be a time when you have engaged additional adult support. You will not be expected to be able to plan provision to accommodate every aspect of need that might affect children's development and learning. However, you should be familiar with those needs that are most familiar and know where to seek guidance and advice, for example your local authority advisory service or your health visitor.

Effective early communication, language and literacy opportunities (S22, S15 and S16)

The way that you promote babies, toddlers and young children's language and communication development, and the ways that you model and promote ways to effectively provide sensitive feedback and encourage sustained shared thinking, will need explaining in your EYPS assessments. Speaking and Listening is a national priority. There has been much research into this area – the original document *Progression in Phonics* was produced by the DfEE for the National Literacy strategy (2000) and was aimed at children in the foundation stage. The *Playing with Sounds* (DfES, 2004d) document which was produced in 2004 as a supplement to this publication gave practical suggestions of activities for developing children's 'sound awareness'. More recently, the Primary National Strategy's new phonics resource *Letters and Sounds: Principles and Practice of High Quality Phonics* (DCSF, 2007a) replaces *Progression in Phonics* and *Playing with Sounds*.

Research in the field of developmental psychology has shown us that there are links between speech, language and communication with learning, behaviour, social skills and children's self-esteem. 'Babies' brains develop at an astonishing pace in the early years. Brains are genetically wired at birth, but the complex circuitry that permits mature thought processes to occur only begins to develop in early childhood and connections continue to be made throughout life and are shaped by experience' (David et al., 2003: 120). EYPs must therefore show how they support their colleagues to understand how babies, toddlers and young children's listening, speaking, pre-reading and pre-writing skills develop. 'It is important for practitioners to know about the biological, social, and cultural development of children and the subject knowledge of what is involved in literacy, so that they can learn how to put the two together to help children learn to read and write' (Bruce and Spratt, 2008: 13).

Early communication, language and literacy, play and learning activities should be fun. As a leader your setting should be bursting with opportunities for baby babble, talking, listening, singing, rhyming and story telling. 'These are the building blocks of literacy and make the difference to how quickly and easily they acquire language' (Brock and Rankin, 2008: 7).

Reflective Activity

Consider the ways that you promote the key aspects illustrated below by Whitehead (1996) in *The Development of Language and Literacy* to others?

✓ Children are sensitive and social communicators from birth.
✓ Children's language is original and creative and enables them to get things done, gain cooperation of others, and comment on their world.
✓ Language is one of the major developments of infancy and, alongside play and other ways of representing experiences like dancing, singing and painting, shapes thinking, learning and literacy.
✓ Speaking and listening must be at the heart of all our provision for care and education in the years 0–8.
✓ Conversations with interested adults are essential to children's linguistic, emotional, social and cognitive welfare.
✓ Early years carers and educators can learn more about their children by observing them and listening to them. In order to do this, we can keep brief notebooks, word diaries, audio and video records, and photographs.

Look at the EYPS standards:

⇒ S10, S15, S16, S22

Communication, Language and Literacy in the EYFS

Communication, Language and Literacy in the EYFS (DCSF, 2008d) is made up of the following aspects:

- Language for Communication
- Language for Thinking
- Linking Sounds and Letters

- Reading
- Writing
- Handwriting.

Your assessor will need to know the ways in which you lead and make provision to promote all babies', toddlers' and young children's communication, language and literacy. You will need to show how you make provision for children who have learning and communication difficulties or disabilities or English as a second language. The way that you make personalized provision to meet children's individual language and communication needs, may have involved you asking a parent or carer to provide you with the basic signs or language that the child uses at home. You may also have examples of working with colleagues from another agency in order make personalized provision. The inclusive nature of early years provision will be explored in more detail in Chapter 6.

Reflective Activity

Language for Communication is about how children become communicators. Learning to listen and speak emerges out of non-verbal communication, which includes facial expression, eye contact and hand gesture (DCSF, 2008d).

How do you practise and encourage others to develop babies, toddlers and young children's ability to:

✓ interact verbally and non-verbally with their peers?
✓ listen carefully to adults and their peers?
✓ extend their vocabulary?
✓ engage in story time?
✓ listen and talk about stories, songs, poems and rhymes?

Look at the EYPS standard:

⇒ S15

Leading effective 'language for communication' practice involves supporting your colleagues to understand ways to challenge children's thinking or in the words of Professor Ferre Laevers, 'looking at the world through the eyes of the child'.

Reflective Activity

Language for Thinking is about how children learn to use language to imagine and recreate roles and experiences, and how they use talk to clarify their thinking and ideas or to refer to events they have observed or are curious about (DSCF, 2008d).

Identify how you lead practice or model ways for babies, toddlers or young children to express themselves verbally or non-verbally:

✓ What is going on in their imagination?
✓ What are they thinking?
✓ In what ways do they put across their ideas?
✓ What has been going on in their lives?
✓ What interests them?
✓ What are their likes and dislikes?
✓ What have they seen?

Look at the EYPS standard: ⇒ S16

The EYPS National Standard S16 refers to the ways in which you model, support and lead the development of babies, toddlers and young children's thinking skills. You will need to show the ways in which you plan and provide both planned and unplanned play and learning opportunities that encourage sustained, shared thinking. While working for Kent Local Authority, I acted as a facilitator at the Hundred Languages of Children exhibition held in the county (Reggio Children, 2000). The exhibition offered early years practitioners the opportunity to look at the experiences of the pre-schools of Reggio Emilia, Italy. Laurence Malaguzzi strongly believed that children are thought to have at least 100 languages – art, music, dance, building, writing, talking, singing, etc. are all considered part of the 100 languages of children. The multiple languages are used to help children build knowledge and understand the world around them. The key message for me is that to engage in sustained shared thinking with babies, toddlers and young children, you need to 'tune in' to the interests of the child and engage in the thought processes connected to the activity that the child is engrossed in, albeit painting, model making, socio-dramatic play or mark making.

Reflective Activity

Sustained shared thinking

- In the most effective settings, practitioners support and challenge children's thinking by getting involved in the thinking process with them.
- Sustained shared thinking involves the adult being aware of the children's interests and understandings and the adult and children working together to develop an idea or skill.
- Sustained shared thinking can only happen when there are responsive trusting relationships between adults and children.
- The adult shows genuine interest, offers encouragement, clarifies ideas and asks open questions. This supports and extends the children's thinking and helps children to make connections in learning.

Source: The Early Years Foundation Stage (DSFC, 2008b), Section 4.3 Learning and Development – Creativity and Critical Thinking.

Use your EYPS reflective log to record the times:

1. that you have engaged in sustained thinking with babies, toddlers and young children
2. led and supported others to engage in sustained thinking with babies, toddlers and young children.

Look at the EYPS standard:

⇒ S16

As with all the areas associated with Communication, Language and Literacy in the EYFS (2007), (DCSF, 2008b) the way that you lead effective practice must be reflected in the way that you encourage adult-initiated and child-initiated play opportunities. 'Evidence from both REPPE and EPPE has suggested that involvement in sustained shared thinking, or what Bruner (1983, 1996) called "joint involvement episodes", may be especially valuable in terms of child development in the early years' (Pugh and Duffy, 2006: 172).

Linking sounds and letters is about how children develop the ability to distinguish between sounds and become familiar with rhyme, rhythm and alliteration (DCSF, 2007a). Leading effective practice here means that there may have been times that you have developed other practitioners' understanding about the relationship between spoken and written sounds. Children's ears need 'tuning in' before they can be expected to work with sounds in words and use letters. There has been much debate about the teaching and learning of phonics. 'It is very useful to have

An EYP candidate engaging in sustained shared thinking with babies

knowledge about phonics and to be able to articulate this to colleagues. The advice in Letters and Sounds is that you should know how to blend and segment clearly yourself, so that you can ensure that you are doing this correctly with children' (Brock and Rankin, 2008).

I feel that letter sounds should be introduced carefully – letters don't make sounds, we make them, and yet, we point to a letter shape and ask a child, using letter shapes 'What sound does it make?'. Role modelling and leading learning in the early years must be fun, so be wary of working with visual letter shapes as potentially it can stop children listening – for example, the letter 'C' used in words like Charlotte, Christopher and cheese all begin with the letter C but all begin with a different phonic sound which can cause confusion and lead children to 'switch off' to that aspect of learning.

Reading is about fostering babies, toddlers and young children's understanding and enjoyment of stories, books and rhymes – they need to understand that 'print carries meaning, both fiction and fact, and reading a range of familiar words and simple sentences' (DCSF 2008d). Your role as an EYP is to encourage other practitioners and parents/carers' understanding about how children develop and consolidate their understanding about:

- the purpose of reading
- reading conventions, for example the way to hold a book, turn pages, the direction of the print
- the sounds of letters and phonics
- patterns and shapes in words.

Writing is about how children build an understanding of the relationship between the spoken and written word and how through making marks, drawing and personal writing, children ascribe meaning to text and attempt to write for various purposes (DCSF, 2008d).

Your job as an EYP is to promote a shared understanding about the ways that children develop and learn pre-reading and re-writing skills. Learning experiences for the babies, toddlers and young children need to be developmentally appropriate, meaningful, fun, engaging and active. Traditional methods of sitting children down for long periods of time, giving them worksheets to complete, and encouraging children to learn letters of the alphabet and numbers off by rote are not necessarily perceived as best practice.

As an EYP, you will be aware that some children are not physically capable of sitting still for sustained periods of time and are not developmentally ready to write or read. With regards to undertaking activities that require children to be seated, my rule of thumb has always been one minute for each year of a child's life plus one minute, so for a two-year-old, this is only three minutes.

Handwriting is about the ways in which children's random marks, lines and drawings develop and form the basis of recognizable letters (DCSF, 2007a). To develop children's pre-writing skills, you need to show how you promote an understanding of a child's physical readiness to write and their understanding of the concept and purpose of writing, for example:

- writing conventions – right to left, top to bottom
- stages of development linked to the development of fine motor control
- recognition of letter sounds and shapes
- writing being used to make marks on greeting cards, letters, emails, etc.
- recognition of patterns, sounds and shapes in words.

Reflective Activity

Observe the way that communication, language and literacy promoted in your setting or network, stand aside and observe the practice:

1. How does the setting promote a rich stimulating language environment both indoors and outdoors?
2. What high-quality interactions and sustained shared thinking is occurring between the practitioners and babies, toddlers or young children?

Look at the EYPS standards:

⇒ S1, S6, S11, S15, S16, S26, S27

One of my LA colleagues positively changed his approach to developing children's pre-writing skills by providing a pencilless pencil case resource to support children in developing their fine manipulative skills. The pencilless pencil case was in fact a brightly coloured tool box packed with small everyday objects, for example pegs, buttons, ribbons, miniature playing cards, small world people or paperclips. The pencilless pencil case helped small children to develop their pincer grip and their hand–eye coordination. 'Motivating children to want to learn to read and write is the route to achievement' (Brock and Rankin, 2008: 99). Treasure baskets are another excellent example of providing a purposeful opportunity to develop early communication, language and literacy skills. Documents such as *Letters and Sounds: Principles and Practice of High Quality Phonics* (DCSF 2007a) provides guidance, examples of activities and ways to undertake assessments of children which are all based on research evidence, but remember that EYPs use their graduate studies to review resources offered with an open mind.

Points for Reflection

- ✓ Continually monitor, review and modify observation and assessment arrangements.
- ✓ Articulate your understanding and purpose of the assessment arrangements to your colleagues.
- ✓ Ensure effective training arrangements are in place.
- ✓ Provide continual feedback about babies, toddlers and young children's outcomes to individuals and teams.
- ✓ Provide written or verbal feedback to parents and carers about their child's general progress.
- ✓ Communicate children's outcomes to colleagues, for example those working with the National Curriculum Key Stage 1 framework to ensure smooth transitions for the child.

Further Reading

Brock, A. and Rankin, C. (2008) *Communication, Language and Literacy from Birth to Five*. London: Sage.

Oussoren. R. (2001) *Write Dance: A Progressive Music and Movement Programme for the Development of Pre-Writing and Writing Skills*. London: Paul Chapman Publishing.

Reggio Children (2000) *The Hundred Languages of Children*, 3rd edition. Reggio Emilia: Reggio Children.

Whitehead, M.R. (2004) *Language and Literacy in the Early Years,* 3rd edition. London: Sage.

Useful Websites

Children's Workforce Development Council – www.cwdcouncil.org.uk
Communication, Language and Literacy in the Early Years Foundation Stage – www.
    standards.dfes.gov.uk/eyfs
National Literacy Trust – www.literacytrust.org.uk

CHAPTER 6

PROTECTING EFFECTIVE PRACTICE

This chapter invites you to reflect on the ways that you interpret, implement and evaluate national policies, statutory and non-statutory frameworks and guidance related to the serious nature of protecting children aged 0–5 years. The chapter will explore the EYPS standards S8, S19 and S20 in relation to health and safety and safeguarding children, S12, S18, S21 and S23 in relation to supporting the rights of children (0–5 years) and finally S7, S13, S14 and S17 in relation to children's (0–5 years) behaviour management. It will encourage you to identify ways to keep yourself up to date with the early years national policies, statutory and non-statutory frameworks and guidance that is required for EYPS standard 4. As the content discussed in this chapter impacts, significantly on your own practice and the way that you lead and support others, this chapter should be read in conjunction with chapter 4, 'What is Effective Practice?', and Chapter 5 'Early Years Effective Practice – Assessment Arrangements, Routines and Communication, Language and Literacy'.

Effective Health and Safety and Child Protection

In your EYPS assessments, you will need to show that you have a good working knowledge of policies and procedures related to health and safety and child protection. These areas are significant, and you will need to show how you establish and maintain a safe and secure environment that makes babies, toddlers or young children develop their independence. The EYPS National Standard S5 sets out the health and safety requirements that you will need to know, while S19 is concerned with the ways in which you act on that knowledge appropriately. This section will help you to explore your accountability and consider what evidence you may have to support your Gateway Review, Written Tasks and Setting Visit assessments.

Point to Remember

'The provider must take necessary steps to safeguard and promote the welfare of children'. (DCSF, 2008b).

As with the other standards, while it is recognized that as an EYP you are accountable for the delivery of your own personal effective practice, you must also show how you lead and support your colleagues to promote children's health and safety and physical, mental and emotional well-being. The accountability that you hold for babies, toddlers and young children's health and safety and well-being is paramount. There are many levels associated with promoting effective practice for children's health and safety and physical, mental and emotional well-being. On one level, you are concerned with ensuring that the staff ratios (DCSF, 2008b: Appendix 2) are adequate to ensure safety, and that the needs of the children are met. On another level, you are concerned with ensuring that the indoor and outdoors environment, furniture, play equipment and toys are safe, secure and positioned appropriately for babies, toddlers and young children's development learning and play. On yet another level, you are accountable for the safe storage of medicines and the medical needs of sick children. On a much more serious level, you are accountable for child protection issues and training. As an EYP, you must be up to date with your Local Authority Safeguarding Children Board guidance and procedures. In your EYPS national assessments, you will need to consider how any training that you may have received in the area of child protection has influenced the policies and procedures that you have in place. As it is a principal objective of an EYP to ensure that babies, toddlers and young children are kept safe and protected from harm and neglect, you will need to show how you regularly monitor your own and others' practice to ensure that you continuously comply with the procedures set out in the EYFS statutory framework (2007) (DCSF, 2008b).

Reflective Activity

In what ways have you influenced any of the following child protection procedures in your setting:

✓ Disseminating information from the LA Safeguarding Children Board?
✓ Mentoring and support for a designated child protection officer?
✓ Policies for child protection procedures?
✓ Arranging child protection training?
✓ Keeping others updated about child protection issues?
✓ Ensuring that all colleagues and volunteers have access to a copy of child protection procedures?
✓ Ensuring that everyone understands and knows what to do if they have concerns about a baby, toddler or young child?
✓ Ensuring that all colleagues and volunteers who have contact with babies, toddlers and young children have enhanced CRB disclosures?
✓ Ensuring that new staff/volunteers who have contact with children have enhanced CRB disclosures before they start work?

Look at the EYPS standards:

⇒ S19, 20

The DfES study 'Being Safe and Protected' (David et al., 2007) reported a high level of child abuse amongst babies and young children.

As an EYP you will be supporting your colleagues to build relationships with the children's parents and carers; it is widely accepted that some parents and carers are hard to reach and this may be for a number of reasons. There may be times that your informed judgements make it necessary to engage the support of other agencies to support parents and carers and more fundamentally the needs of the child. Safeguarding children is 'a shared responsibility – shared between parents, carers and agencies. It is inherently charged with high risk, tension and emotion. It involves professionals making finely-balanced judgements about children in very difficult circumstances' (NCB, 2009). Many lessons have been learnt about the tensions that exist between carers and agencies working together to safeguard children, as in the case of Baby P, a 17-month-old boy who died in August 2007 after months of abuse in Haringey, north London. He was in the care of the same Local Authority in which eight-year-old Victoria Climbie was murdered in 2000 by her great aunt and the woman's boyfriend. As a consequence of these deeply tragic incidents, the ramifications for safeguarding practice across the early years sector has impacted significantly on the important role played by an EYP.

Reflection Point

EYPs must ensure that they are aware of the safeguarding Vulnerable Groups Act 2006 and the guidance issued under this act. Duties on providers include:

- employment laws
- anti-discriminatory legislation
- health and safety legislation
- data collection regulations
- duty of care.

In the second Reflective Activity that you undertook in Chapter 3, you started to identify the leadership characteristics that you adopt to lead and support your colleagues to care for children effectively. You will now need to consider how you model and lead others to provide a safe and sound environment (S19) where children are able to engage in risk taking and learn by their mistakes. Babies, toddlers and young children are often curious and need supportive, enabling adults to foster an understanding about dangers posed to them; they need to grow and learn, knowing how to keep themselves safe. Babies, toddlers and young children can get upset or distressed for a number of reasons, for example if they tumble, if they are teething or are in pain, if another child has upset them, if they are having a tantrum or being separated from their parent or carer. Examples of the type of support and comfort that you facilitate amongst your colleagues may be the procedures you have in place when a child starts the setting, the initial meetings that you have with the parent or carer to ascertain information about the child's needs prior to the child starting with you or observing the baby, toddler and young child when they first start, to ensure they settle into the routines and procedures of the setting and feel at ease (S10).

Children In Danger or At Risk (S20)

On a day-to-day operational level, there are risks to babies, toddlers and young children in the physical learning and play environment. Doors and gates need to be locked to ensure that strangers do not wander in or that children do not wander out! Trips and slips can occur if children are not aware of the dangers of steps, water spillages and leaving toys and equipment lying around.

> ### Point to Remember
>
> Outdoor and indoor spaces, furniture, equipment and toys must be safe and suitable for their purpose (DCSF 2008b).

Children love to press the buttons on remote controls and electrical equipment – it never ceases to amaze me how quickly babies learn to crawl and head towards the controls on the television or DVD! Computers, electrical equipment and plug sockets need to be safely concealed and positioned, health and safety risks need to be explained appropriately to children as they move about the environment and access computers and other electrical and ICT aids. The EYP must model appropriately and lead others in the promotion of health and safety and physical, mental and emotional well-being. Risk assessments must be conducted and reviewed. The Statutory Guidance for the EYFS (DCSF 2008a) states that the provider must cover anything that the child comes into contact with. This just about means everything!

> ### Reflective Activity
>
> How do you influence the practice in your setting or network to ensure that:
>
> ✓ the premises and equipment are clean?
> ✓ accidents, hazards and faulty equipment are dealt with appropriately?
> ✓ the health and safety policy is reviewed regularly?
> ✓ records of risk assessments are maintained?
>
> **Look at the EYPS standard:**
>
> ⇒ S19

Healthy Meals, Snacks and Drinks

As healthy eating and the promotion of regular physical exercise are part of the EYFS, you may discuss your role in promoting healthy, balanced and nutritious meals and snacks and drinks in your assessments.

Reflective Activity

How do you keep your knowledge up to date and promote meals, snacks and drinks that:

- ✓ provide a healthy, balanced and nutritious diet?
- ✓ provide access to fresh drinking water at all times?
- ✓ are suited to a child's dietary needs and allergies?
- ✓ take account of children's likes and dislikes?
- ✓ are prepared in accordance with the Local Authority Environmental Health department?
- ✓ are stored safely?

Look at the EYPS standards:

⇒ S5, S19

Point to Remember

'The provider must promote the good health of the children, take necessary steps to prevent the spread of infection and take appropriate actions when they are ill' (DCSF, 2008b: 19).

In setting up a new baby care unit, in my role as head of a nursery unit located on an FE college site, I held responsibility for the health and safety of the babies, toddlers and young children and my team of early years colleagues. I can remember that as part of the initial planning meeting, while working collaboratively with my colleagues to draw up the plans for the building, I listened to their views and paid attention to every detail. This resulted in me negotiating with the architect to include essential defined areas for nappy changing and disposal of soiled items, and a separate milk kitchen with a separate fridge to store and prepare the babies' feeds. As an EYP, you must be aware of the impact of the working environment upon the well-being of your colleagues, which in turn affects their attitude to the work and their approach to the babies, toddlers and young children. When setting up the nursery, I insisted that my colleagues had their own rest room away from the children so that they could relax, recharge their batteries and have time out to reflect on their own practice. The new nursery was a far cry from the old mobile unit that was tucked away at the back of the college and quite rightly became one of the most celebrated areas in the college.

Case Study of the Healthy Eating Activity Undertaken by an EYP Candidate on her 0–20 Month Placement

While attending my placement, I became familiar with the babies' routine and got to know some of the babies. During one visit, I witnessed an 11-month-old child being fed lunch consisting of a sausage roll, two slices of processed cheese and a slice of processed ham. The lunch was sent in from home. I expressed my concern at the high levels of salt and processed food being given to the baby and the practitioners agreed that the nutritional needs of this child were not being met. The practitioners explained that they had tried hard to persuade the baby's mother to change the type of food she supplies for her child but had had no success.

I discussed the importance of the food supplied by parents with the Manager and how the nursery has a responsibility to ensure the child receives nutritious food. We agreed that it was a sensitive issue that needed to be handled carefully. The Manager asked me about how lunchtime works at my setting. I talked about how I had made a policy of not allowing packed lunches as I have neither the space nor equipment (fridges) to be able to cater for them. All children who stay over the lunch period have a home-cooked, setting lunch. I suggested that she start to tackle this problem by putting a leaflet together detailing the importance of giving healthy, nutritious food to young babies and highlighting the long-term health implications for those children who are given foods high in salt and sugar. I also suggested that she put menu suggestions together to give parents ideas of how to make up a healthy packed lunch. I organized a workshop for the parents concerning the provision of healthy packed lunches. As the setting provided a hot cooked lunch for toddlers and young children who wish to take it up, I suggested that the Manager promote this option to the parents in the baby unit, emphasizing that it would save them time in the mornings and they would feel good in the knowledge that their child was receiving a hot, nutritious meal at lunchtime. I discussed ways of broaching this sensitive topic, emphasizing the importance of making the idea available to all parents so as not to single out one parent in particular.

I would like to think that my discussions with the Manager of the setting were beneficial in that I helped her resolve her predicament with a parent providing unsuitable food for a baby. I believe she felt more confident about tackling the problem knowing how another setting would deal with the problem.

Look at the EYPS standards:

⇒ S1, S13, S19, S20, S24, S29

Point for Reflection

The EYPS standard 35 asks you to show how you influence and shape the policies and practices in the setting and share in collective responsibility for their implementation. Consider ways that you have influenced policies and practices related to health and safety. For example, you may have influenced a 'sick child' policy in your setting, which outlines the actions to be taken by your colleagues when a baby, toddler or young child is ill and provides information about the necessary steps to prevent infection.

Children's Rights, Inclusion and Anti-discriminatory Practice

To promote babies, toddlers and young children's rights, inclusion and anti-discriminatory practice, you must lead, model and practise the way in which to treat all children fairly, irrespective of their race, ethnicity, culture, religion, gender, sexual orientation, family background, learning difficulties and/or disabilities.

This may sound like something that comes naturally, but meeting these needs is highly complex and requires you to be constantly watchful and receptive. There are clear examples to support you in meeting children's individual needs outlined in the EYFS framework (DCSF, 2008b) and in the Practice Guidance to the EYFS (DCSF, 2008b). 'Children learn best when they are healthy, safe and secure, when their individual needs are met and when they have positive relationships with the adults caring for them. The welfare requirements are designed to support providers in creating a setting which is welcoming, safe and stimulating, and where children are able to enjoy themselves, to grow in confidence and to fulfil their potential' (DCSF, 2008a).

Written Activity

Read the EYFS Effective Practice: Inclusive Practice document (DCSF, 2007) – it can be accessed on the internet at:
www.standards.dcsf.gov.uk/eyfs/resources/downloads/1_2_ep.pdf

1. Record examples of the ways in which you have practised and promoted ways to make inclusive personalized provision for children (aged 0–5 years).
2. Explain how you monitor whether or not children's (aged 0–5 years) needs are being met and if they are confident, happy and engaged in learning.

3.   Include examples of making personalized provision for children's:

  • race, ethnicity, culture
  • religion
  • gender/sexual orientation
  • family background
  • learning difficulties and/or disabilities.

Consider how your experience relates to the EYPS standards:

⇒ S13, S18, S21

In your assessments, you will need to explain how you promote early identification of babies, toddlers or young children's individual needs. To help you reflect on this process, look at Figure 5.1 in the previous chapter. You may consider, for example, providing an example of a time that you sought advice from a colleague working in LA specialist support services (S6). Consider using an example of a time that you have made provision for children from ethnic minority backgrounds or for a child with a learning difficulty and/or disability, and how it involved you and your colleagues adapting activities or environments, providing alternative activities, or using specialist aids and equipment.

An EYP candidate leading practitioners to develop their signing skills

Case Study of an EYP Candidate Working Collaboratively with an Early Years Specialist Support Teacher

Context:

Tom, who has language delay, attends the nursery for one and a half days a week. Tom is already on the Early Support Programme and also receives Portage, a home-based service for parents to help to develop their child's skills. He is a very happy child but has no spoken language at all. He also attends another setting and is starting to use signing there. To support Tom's needs, I liaised with the Pre-school Specialist Teacher to arrange an Introduction to Makaton Signing so that all the practitioners at my setting could support Tom's communication skills.

The training delivered was devised in partnership with the Pre-school Specialist Teacher and me. The strategies devised included introducing 20 basic signs for all the practitioners to use with Tom and all the other children, some additional signs for specific activities and areas of learning, for example the concepts of 'big and small' and question words which are within the Problem Solving, Reasoning and Numeracy Area of Learning. Practitioners were also introduced to the manual alphabet, to sign the first letter of the child's name whilst talking to them or saying hello/goodbye, and some songs/nursery rhymes to use with the whole group.

The Pre-school Specialist Teacher ensured that the staff members had a lot of practice saying and signing each word to help them gain in confidence, but I also gave them sentences to sign to demonstrate how signing can be used on a daily basis.

As an Individual Education Plan (IEP) is a requirement of the Special Educational Needs Code of Practice (DfES, 2001; 2002) and is essential and crucial evidence if the setting or parents wish to request that the Local Authority carry out a Statutory Assessment of Tom's needs, I sat with Tom's key worker and discussed suitable IEP targets. I continually reviewed and monitored his IEP targets with his key worker and discussed the progress made with the Pre-school Specialist Teacher on her visits.

I continued to model the target words in everyday practice and signed other words to Tom. This High/Scope process of plan–do–review continued throughout the year and is reflected in my Pre-school Specialist Teacher notes of visit form.

Tom is now starting to use a small number of single words, so I adjusted his current IEP target to support his saying a single word alongside the signing.

Look at the EYPS standards:

⇒ S6, S14, S15, S18, S19, S23, S31

The government's Early Support programme (DCSF, 2008e) is designed to deliver improved services for parents and carers of young disabled children. It offers advice and guidance which you may have accessed in providing support for families with disabled children.

In my role as a Local Authority Advisory Teacher, I led an initiative based on the 'Index for Inclusion' (Booth et al., 2006). The Index for Inclusion initiative was designed to support practitioners to identify ways of engaging governors, staff, parents and children (aged 0–5 years) in all aspects of inclusive practice. My role involved me liaising with the governors, the children, the parents/carers, curriculum leaders, other practitioners and any volunteers working in the setting. I supported a review of the inclusiveness of the setting's culture, policy and practices using the Index for Inclusion. In feeding back the outcomes of the reviews, I would recommend that the setting seek the support of specialist early years professionals, for example the Travelers service, the Special Educational Needs Advisor or the Speech and Language service. I encouraged others to consider the inclusiveness of the setting, the resources and identify any barriers to children's (aged 0–5 years) care, learning and play experiences. I supported the nominated leader, in each setting that I worked in, to identify key action points that would assist inclusive practices and to write a development plan with SMART goals which was implemented and reviewed periodically. Following the initial assessment, the EYP role would be to monitor and ensure that the action plan was sustained and, more importantly, to check that it was making a difference to the children.

Reflective Activity

To show how you promote positive attitudes to diversity and difference with children and adults, consider recording examples in your EYP reflective log of the ways that you have worked collaboratively with your colleagues to plan activities that have helped children learn about and value the differences in their peers and other people's lives. For example, you may have examples of taking the lead in organizing festivals and events that encourage children to acquire an appreciation of and respect for their own and other children's cultures in a way that promotes tolerance of other traditions and lifestyles.

Look at the EYPS standards:

⇒ S18, S12

Children's Rights

Being an EYP means that you sign up to being an advocate for children's rights and that you actively promote equality of opportunity and anti-discriminatory practice to your colleagues, parents and carers.

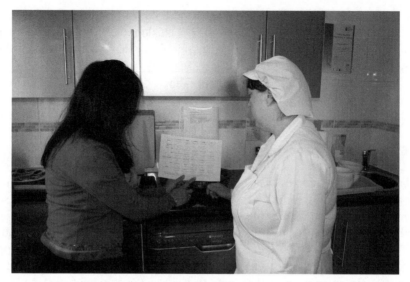

An EYP discussing the individual dietary needs of the children

'All children have a legal right to be treated equally and not suffer discrimination.' The United Nations Convention on the Rights of the Child (1989), which has been ratified by the UK, gives children from birth important rights and entitlements. The appointment of the first children's commissioner for England and Wales in 2005 adds weight to the importance of children's rights. The UK also has strong laws to ensure that all children are treated equally and should not suffer discrimination on the grounds of race or gender. Early childhood practitioners are required by law to provide equal access to their services and adopt inclusive, anti-discriminatory practices (Bruce, 2006: 66).

✓ All children are citizens and have rights and entitlements.
✓ Children should be treated fairly, regardless of race, religion or abilities.
✓ This applies no matter:

- what they think or say
- what type of family they come from
- what language(s) they speak
- what their parents do
- whether they are girls or boys
- whether they have a disability
- whether they are rich or poor.

✓ All children have an equal right to be listened to and valued in the setting.

Points for Reflection

Children's Rights and entitlements

✓ How do you promote children's rights in your setting or network?
✓ Have you influenced a children's rights policy or charter in your setting or network; if so, is it accessible to children, governors, management committees, colleagues, parents and carers?
✓ Have you included a statement about children's rights in your setting information pack?
✓ Do you display children's rights on your parent notice board?
✓ How do you monitor whether or not children's rights are upheld?

Look at the EYPS standard:

⇒ S18

Being an EYP means that you must protect children's rights in the context of Every Child Matters and anti-discriminatory legislation – there are many social inequalities that exist in our society today and by being accountable for the delivery of the ECM agenda, it means that you are playing a key role in addressing the balance and eradicating inequalities. By showing how you have used development tools such as the Index for Inclusion (Booth, et al., 2006), the CAF or the government's Early Support programme (DCSF, 2008e), you will be able to demonstrate how you support, monitor and evaluate your own or your colleagues' inclusive practices and facilitate the removal of any barriers that may exist for children's well-being, learning and development.

Reflective Activity

Reflect on the ways in which you have influenced the provision of a safe and supportive inclusive learning environment where babies, toddlers and young children feel:

✓ free from harassment
✓ valued for who they are
✓ that discriminatory expressions and prejudices are challenged.

Look at the EYPS standards:

⇒ S18, S12, S23

High Expectations of Children

I believe that there are a number of interconnecting influences that affect our ability to learn and develop – as a human species, we need:

- ✓   our personal, social and emotional needs to be met
- ✓   to be understood as individuals
- ✓   to feel at ease with who we are
- ✓   to have our efforts recognized
- ✓   to be supported by enabling others.

In your assessments, you will need to show, firstly, how you model and promote ways to recognize that every child is special, despite their different strengths and abilities and their different stage of development (S13). Secondly, you will need to show how you model and promote a culture that sets 'high expectations' (S7) for all children (aged 0–5 years) and helps them reach their full potential. Finally, you will need to show how you model and promote ways to support individual children's learning and behaviour (S17). Questions that you may advise your colleagues to use when seeking information from parents, carers (S29–S32) or other professionals (S6) include:

- •   What makes this child unique and special?
- •   What are their needs?
- •   What are their likes and dislikes?
- •   What are their strengths?
- •   What are their weaknesses?
- •   Where do they live and what is their family background?
- •   Have they got any learning difficulties or disabilities?
- •   Is English their second language?
- •   What are their cultural and religious needs?

Working in partnership with parents and carers will be discussed in more detail in the next chapter, Chapter 7. Remember that the way you use observational assessments (S10) to paint a pen portrait of the child discussed previously will also help you to meet standard S18 – 'Promote children's rights, equality and inclusion and anti-discriminatory practice' (CWDC, 2008b) in all aspects – to inform your effective practice.

Reflective Activity

Consider how you practise personally and promote to others effective ways to:

✓ gather relevant information about the individual children's (aged 0–5 years) needs, their home background and circumstances, their levels of development and past achievements?
✓ involve parents, carers and other professionals to gather this information?
✓ combine the information you gather from parents, carers and other professionals with observational assessments to plan for the next steps in children's (aged 0–5 years) development and learning?

Look at the EYPS standards:

⇒ S7, S10, S18

Behaviour Management

Your graduate studies will have informed your understanding about the development of children's (aged 0–5 years) social and emotional skills and the adverse effect that can occur when children are prevented from developing these. When children are denied the opportunity to develop emotionally and socially, it affects their ability to feel safe and secure, to play freely, and to become responsible for their own actions, their decisions and any mistakes that they may make. In my experience of supporting practitioners to develop appropriate behaviour management strategies for young children (aged 0–5 years), I have often observed practitioners referring to children as 'mischievous' or 'naughty' and even 'behaviourally challenged'. I have a strong viewpoint on this as, more often than not, these children were using their behaviour to cry for help, to cover up the fact that they did not understand what was expected of them or that they were being asked to do something that is far beyond their level of ability. Children displaying signs of poor behaviour need your support and careful handling, as they can be ostracized by their peers who cannot understand why they are behaving so badly and are frightened of getting hurt themselves.

> The places where we work provide a safe place outside the home, where we can start to explore relationships; children and young people need help in understanding that their own behaviour and what they do and the ways in which they act will be felt by others. They learn how to make and keep friends, how to resist doing the wrong thing and how to know what is the right thing to do. (Overall, 2007: 105)

In your assessments, you will need to show how you model and promote ways to find out the underlying cause of poor behaviour, which can sometimes go beyond the setting, and seek solutions. Early intervention can nip potential behavioural problems in the bud – for example, I once worked alongside a LA SENCO to support a key worker in designing a behaviour modification programme in consultation with his mother for a child who was displaying disruptive tendencies. For your EYPS national assessments, you will need to use concrete examples of the ways in which you have offered support and advice to your colleagues, parents and carers, for example to challenge a stereotypical viewpoint, or to raise expectations about a particular child, or to remove a barrier for a child's participation and attainment.

The EYPS standard S17 requires you to show how you practise, model and lead effective behaviour management strategies, using your knowledge and understanding about how children's (aged 0–5 years) social and emotional development can influence their behaviour. To do this, you will need to demonstrate how you have used your knowledge to influence, design and plan or implement developmentally appropriate behaviour management strategies, policies or procedures for children (aged 0–5 years). Remember that these should all give the children (aged 0–5 years) the opportunity to develop self-control and independence, irrespective of their ethnicity, culture or religion, home language, family background, learning difficulties and/or disabilities, gender or ability.

 Key Points

'Children's behaviour must be managed effectively and in a manner appropriate for their stages of development and particular needs' (DCSF, 2008b).

Consider ways in which you can influence a fair and consistent approach to behaviour management in the setting, for example:

- manage behaviour on a daily basis
- reinforce positive behaviour
- praise children for their good behaviour
- provide constructive feedback
- use assertive skills to challenge unacceptable behaviour
- identify poor behaviour that has excluded or ostracized a child
- prevent the attention of the poor behaviour to the detriment of the group
- follow up children's poor behaviour promptly
- work in partnership with parents, carers and other professionals to manage behavioural difficulties
- design and implement a behaviour modification plan

- influence a behaviour management policy and strategies
- set realistic strategies and expectations for children's behaviour
- establish clear rules and boundaries
- encourage children's (aged 0–5 years) ability to become respectful of their peers and adults
- encourage children to resolve their own conflicts.

Look at the EYPS standards:

⇒ S17, S14

Further Reading

Booth, T., Ainscow, M. and Kingston, D. (2006) *Index for Inclusion: Developing Play, Learning and Participation in Early Years and Childcare*. Bristol: Centre for Studies on Inclusive Education.

Overall, L. (2007) *Supporting Children's Learning*. London: Sage.

United Nations (1989) *Convention on the Rights of the Child*. New York: United Nations.

Useful Websites

Early Childhood Forum (leaflet) 'Participation and belonging in early years settings – inclusion: working towards equality'; available online from the Aims and Principles page of the Early Childhood Forum – www.ncb.org.uk/ecf (see link below 'Inclusion statement')

Early Support (2004) *Early Support Family Pack*. Nottingham: DfES Publications. Available online from the Materials page of the Early Support website – www.early support.org.uk

Early Support (2005) *Family File*. Nottingham: DfES Publications. Available online from the Materials page of the Early Support website – www.earlysupport.org.uk

KIDSactive/SureStart (2004) *All of Us: Inclusion Checklist for Settings*. Nottingham: DfES Publications. Available online from the Publications page of SureStart – www. surestart.gov.uk/publications

CHAPTER 7

RELATIONSHIPS WITH CHILDREN, FAMILIES AND CARERS

This chapter will support EYPs' understanding of the EYPS national standards 29–32 – 'Communicating and working in partnership with parents' – by exploring ways in which the EYP can lead, model and establish ways to recognize and respect the influences and contribution that parents and carers can make to children's development, well-being and learning. It will also look at ways to provide formal and informal opportunities through which information about children's (aged 0–5 years) well-being, development and learning can be shared between the parents and the setting. The chapter will then go on to examine how EYPs can lead, model and establish fair, respectful, trusting, supportive and constructive relationships with children in relation to the EYPS standards 25–28 – 'Relationships with children'.

Working in Partnership with Parents and Carers

'The *Children's Plan – Building Brighter Futures* (2008) aims to make England the best place in the world for children and young people to grow up in' (DCSF, 2007b). EYPs will be part of making the government aspiration happen by signing up to support the five principles that underpin the plan:

✓ The government does not bring up children – parents do – so the government needs to do more to back the parents.

✓ All children have the potential to succeed and should go as far as their talents can take them.

✓ Children and young people need to enjoy their childhood as well as grow up prepared for adult life.

✓ Services need to be shaped by and be responsive to children, young people and families, not designed around professional boundaries.

✓ It is always better to prevent failure rather than tackle a crisis later (DCSF, 2007b: 5).

Depending on your profession, for example childminders, pre-school workers, children's centre workers or local authority advisors, the way that you lead and support others to effectively communicate with children, parents and carers will vary depending on the type of setting, network or the advisory service that you work in. Your graduate studies will have developed your sound understanding of the important influence that a child's home background has on their learning and development. 'The Pen Green Centre for under 5s in Corby, England and the Reggio Emillio pre-schools and infant–toddler centres in Italy are excellent examples of settings where parents and practitioners have developed and engaged in powerful relationships' (Rodd, 2006: 225). Parents being the experts on their own children's learning is one of the principles that underpins these approaches, which compares favourably to the first principle of the children's plan (DCSF, 2007b) – 'the government does not bring up children – parents do'. These approaches involve parents/carers in their children's development by:

✓ providing training opportunities

✓ spending time with parents to help them understand how their children learn and develop

✓ encouraging parents to spend time observing their children engaging in activities in the setting

✓ encouraging parents to share their child's experiences at home with practitioners

✓ ensuring that children's records are shared between the parent/carer and the practitioner.

Point for Reflection

'The parents learned from observing their children and developed an appreciation of their children's high levels of achievements at home with confidence, clarity and joy ... The children have been primarily beneficiaries of this collaboration between parents and practitioners. We all had valuable knowledge and understanding to share. This was a group which enjoyed mutual respect, shared understandings, political awareness and a commitment to extending learning opportunities for young children.' (Parker, 2002: 92–3 in Nutbrown, 2006)

In your EYPS assessments, you will need to demonstrate that you understand and lead effective ways of working in partnership with parents/carers in order to develop children's well-being, development and learning. This will involve showing how you personally develop and sustain effective partnerships and relationships with parents and the ways in which you promote it to others. The previous chapter highlighted the importance of promoting ways to communicate effectively with parents to find out information about the child's needs and interests in the course of making personalized provision for the child (S13).

Communicating with Parents and Carers

To communicate effectively with parents/carers, it sometimes means that you have to sensitively acknowledge the demands made upon the modern-day family. 'Whilst the idea that parents should play a major role in their children's learning now passes virtually uncontested, any family involvement must be at the families' own pace and way' (Whalley et al., 2008). EYPs will understand these demands and communicate these to their colleagues so that they too can appreciate the hectic lifestyles and seek ways to put parents at ease. I have not come across a working parent who has not felt guilty at some point in their career for placing their child in care, despite the high level of skills and expertise that practitioners hold. I am truly indebted to the childminders and practitioners who supported and shared in the learning and development of my two lovely daughters. I believe I would not have reached this stage in my career, or even be writing this book if I had not been supported as a working mum by excellent childcare practictioners. Communicating with parents and carers is a two-way process and you will need to show how you make the most of your skills to develop protocols that ensure both parties are valued and respected and feel at ease while discussing issues concerning the child, as well as being able to communicate effectively with parents/carers.

One study involving coordinators, managers and owners of early childhood centres or settings across the UK found that 22 per cent of the leader's time was spent in contact with parents and other professionals (Muijs et al., 2004) – that is over one fifth of your time dedicated to developing and sustaining professional relationships. In developing relationships with parents and carers, EYPs must show how they are positive, and respectful of their cultural background, religious belief or ethnicity. You may also need to explain how you use your interpersonal skills of empathy, sensitivity and confidentiality to communicate with parents/carers in your EYPS assessments. The ways that you lead and support your colleagues, communicate, establish and maintain positive and effective relationships with parents will also need to be shown in your EYPS assessments.

Reflective Activity

Identify examples of times that you have coached your colleagues in ways to:

✓ provide welcoming surroundings and an atmosphere where parents feel at ease
✓ provide formal and informal opportunities to exchange information about their child's well-being, learning and development, progress and achievements
✓ establish with parents an effective two-way flow of information
✓ recognize when parents need support in nurturing their children
✓ work in partnership with parents in order to improve outcomes for children.

(Adapted from CWDC Guidance to Standards (2008b))

Look at the EYPS standards:

⇒ S29, S30, S31, S32

'Communication practices are the key to successfully negotiating relationships with parents' (Hughes and MacNaugton, 2002 in Rodd, 2006: 229). Their recommendations for fostering partnerships and a shared understanding with parents include to:

✓ explain issues clearly and unambiguously
✓ remain non-judgemental
✓ overcome stereotypical views and/or attitudes
✓ listen and acknowledge feelings
✓ respond in ways that will enhance relationships
✓ manage personal feelings
✓ express viewpoints professionally
✓ confidently assert professional judgements
✓ recognize and respond to conflict appropriately
✓ involve parents as active and equal partners in decision making.

Working in Partnership

CWDC (2008b) also advise that EYPs need to show in their assessments how they 'work to create and sustain opportunities to involve parents as active partners in their children's well-being, learning and development' EYPS Standards 29–32, 53–59.)

Points for Reflection

In your role of leading effective practice, answer the questions from EYFS document 'Effective Practice: Parents as Partners' (DSEF, 2007):

- ✓ How does your setting involve parents in partnership?
- ✓ What opportunities are there for parents to contribute to practitioners' developing understanding of the child as a unique individual?
- ✓ Do you have information around the setting which makes the process of learning visible for all parents and children?
- ✓ Do parents understand your policies on important areas such as key person, inclusion, behaviour, learning and teaching? Have they been involved in drawing them up?
- ✓ Have you ever started a joint project with parents when both they and practitioners were researching children's learning?
- ✓ Do you support parents in developing their own skills and understanding so that they might be better able to support their child's learning?
- ✓ How do parents contribute to planning the learning environment?
- ✓ Are parents encouraged to evaluate the environment with their child's needs and interests in mind?

Look at the EYPS standard:

⇒ S31

The ECM agenda offers parents the opportunity to work by providing accessible, affordable childcare – while there are fully funded places available for children, government tax credit initiatives for parents make up the shortfall by paying for the additional hours. Many parents work long and demanding hours and are reliant on childcare provision that meets both their own needs and their children's. In supporting the costs of childcare, parents may not be available for you to talk to. Innovative ways of keeping parents informed about their child's progress need to be fostered. One setting that I visited as an Early Years advisory teacher used a web-based video recorder that parents could log in to using a protected password while at work. 'Parents need to know what goes on day to day in the nursery so they don't get confused or panicked by what they hear in the media these days' (a quote from a Manager in a day nursery, in Rodd, 2006: 222).

Reflective Activity

Identify examples of times that you have encouraged or coached your colleagues to:

- ✓ organize outings and events to which parents are invited in order to build and maintain relationships

✓ set up a parent notice board or community display board to which parents can contribute

✓ invite parents in to explain and celebrate aspects of their culture, such as music or food

✓ involve older members of a family in remembering aspects of life in the past or families who originate from a different country with differences in culture.

(Adapted from CWDC Guidance to Standards (2008b))

Look at the EYPs standards:

⇒ S29, S31

The Effective Provision of Pre-School education (EPPE) project found that the most effective settings were the ones that had developed:

✓ strong relationships with their parents
✓ positive contact with their parents and carers
✓ ways to share information with their parents and carers
✓ educational aims which were shared with parents/carers
✓ involvement of parents/carers in decision making about their child's learning.

Rodd (2006: 220) suggests that 'parent involvement and programmes for parents form a core part of early childhood service and delivery, and periodic interests have been shown in themes of:

✓ partnership (a philosophy of shared child rearing)
✓ continuity (the promotion of consistency between the conditions and experiences of setting and home)
✓ parent education (the professional responsibility to support and educate parents to enhance children's well-being, parental enjoyment and competence in the parental role)'.

I have personally run various initiatives aimed at developing parents' understanding about the way that their baby, toddler or young child learns and develops. Very often, I would encourage parents to participate in the activities set up in the pre-school for their children. I have always been overwhelmed by the gratitude that the parents have shown at the end of such events. As a trainer, it is important for me to gauge the level of delivery to the level of the parent's comprehension and learning, style. Parents who are not involved in the early years sector cannot be expected to know as much as we do about child development and learning, as indeed we cannot know about their professional roles and interests. Parents/carers are influenced by the media, other parents and society as a whole, and there are very mixed messages about the ways that children should approach their learning. Parents/carers have often thanked me for sharing with them suggestions about the types of activities that are developmentally appropriate for their child.

Reflective Activity

Identify how you support your colleagues to communicate and work in partnership with families and carers, for example do you:

- ✓ coach your colleagues to summarize information from monitoring and assessments and use this information as a basis for discussion with parents?
- ✓ make arrangements for working parents?
- ✓ shadow colleagues on home visits, or during discussions in the setting, giving feedback to them in order to consolidate or improve their skills?
- ✓ demonstrate how to run workshops, formal and informal meetings and conferences?
- ✓ model how to conduct interviews with parents on sensitive issues?

(Adapted from CWDC Guidance to Standards (2008b))

Look at the EYPS standards:

⇒ S29, S30, S31, S32

Relationships with Children

The way that you lead and model practice that fosters long-lasting personal relationships with babies, toddlers and young children relates to EYPS standards 25–28 – 'Relationships with children' (CWDC, 2008b).

Through your own personal practice, you need to show how you set high standards for communicating with children of all ages, backgrounds and abilities.

Central to CWDC (2008a) standards 25–28 is the understanding that your relationship with a baby, toddler or a young child is characterized not only by the way that you talk to them and make clear your expectations of them, but by the way you also listen to them, value and respect what they have to say. By gettting to know them you will 'find out how best to support their learning and development' (p. 46).

Points for Reflection

The way that you offer your support to your colleagues, will differ according to the type of setting that you are working in. Consider the ways in which you support your colleagues' ability to communicate with babies, toddlers and young children, for example:

- ✓ working with babies, toddlers or young children with little or no speech
- ✓ working with babies, toddlers or young children with English as a second language
- ✓ opportunities for colleagues to observe, talk and listen to particular babies, toddlers or children
- ✓ joint evaluation of babies, toddlers or children observations
- ✓ modelling personal skills in listening to and responding positively to children
- ✓ communicating with the baby, toddler or young child at their height, in order to 'look at the world' from their eyes
- ✓ encouraging key workers to find out what interests children have at home or in their local community and encouraging them to share them with other children, or use them as a starting point for talking, play activities or projects and themes.

(Adapted from CWDC Guidance to the Standards (2008b))

Look at the EYPS standards:

⇒ S25, S26, S27, S28

It is important to form positive relationships with babies, toddlers and young children, as research suggests that they secure attachments which are the basis for learning and development.

Rutter's (1995) research suggests that children cope well with having several adults to look after them, as long as it is the same adults over time. Further, children need those people with whom they have a secure attachment relationship to be available at times when they are tired, distressed or facing challenging circumstances.

The link between attachment and learning is made explicit in the study by Mooney and Munton's (1997) review of Howes and Hamilton (1993) and Howes et al. (1994), in as much as secure relationships between caregivers and children can be an important influence on children's behaviour, promoting more advanced types of play and better peer relationships. Colwyn Trevarthen's (1995) work on the development of babies is relevant to thinking about the EYP role and babies, toddlers and young

Key person taking account of the child's interests at an EYP's setting

children's learning. He argues that from their very earliest days, babies are highly motivated to learn. Their learning is profoundly influenced by the interplay or 'proto-conversations' between themselves and their parents and carers. 'In many respects, a childminder is automatically a key person for the children they care for. In an early years setting, it is of course much easier to care for children by teamwork and organizing the key person' (DCSF, 2008a: 57).

   Points for Reflection

In your own personal practice and your leadership of others, how do you:

- ✓ take an interest in babies, toddlers and young children as individuals?
- ✓ treat babies, toddlers and young children fairly and with respect and consideration?
- ✓ appreciate babies, toddlers and young children's cultural diversity?
- ✓ ensure babies, toddlers and young children feel valued?
- ✓ take account of babies, toddlers and young children's skills, interests and preferences?
- ✓ endeavour to make babies, toddlers and young children feel safe and secure and identify changes in babies, toddlers and young children's attitudes or behaviour and follow up any concerns?

✓ apply rules consistently?
✓ ensure you don't embarrass individuals or make them afraid to make mistakes?
✓ listen carefully to them and take account of their responses?
✓ ask open-ended questions to find out what they are thinking and feeling?
✓ involve them and their families in decisions concerning them?

(Adapted from CWDC Guidance to the Standards (2008b.))

Look at the EYPS standard:

⇒ S25

Communicating

As discussed earlier in this chapter in relation to communicating with parents, communication is a two-way process.

> EYPs allow children to initiate and engage in communication at their own pace, and attract the interest and attention of children, using methods appropriate to their age and developmental stage. This means that they provide the space for children to enter into a conversation with them, including those who are reticent or lacking in confidence. (CWDC, 2008b: 49)

You may have come across children who do not wish to communicate or ones who experience a language delay. In your EYPS assessments, you may wish to discuss the ways in which you supported a specific child in overcoming such barriers by seeking the support of other professionals.

Reflective Activity

EYPS S26 asks you to show how you 'Communicate sensitively and effectively with children from birth to the end of the foundation stage' (CWDC, 2008b).

Reflect on the ways that you:

✓ use your knowledge of babies, toddlers and young children's home circumstances, interests and preferences as topics of discussion
✓ use stories, sounds, rhymes, games, gestures, symbols, signs and language-based activities and experiences to communicate effectively

(Continued)

(Continued)

✓ encourage children to communicate in different ways, such as through touch, mark making, pretend play and painting
✓ recognize when a child uses a puppet or imaginary friend to communicate through
✓ recognize when a child may have a communication problem and know where to seek help and advice
✓ differentiate the way that you communicate with babies, toddlers and young children at a level and pace suited to their development and understanding
✓ use both verbal and non-verbal forms of communication to convey meaning, demonstrating that effective communication relies upon more than language
✓ encourage children to communicate respectfully with adults and with each other
✓ help children to use language for negotiating disagreements rather than physical responses.

(Adapted from CWDC Guidance to the Standards (2008b.))

Look at the EYPs standard:

⇒ S26

Listening to Children

Standard 26 describes how EYPs communicate with children whereas S27 is based on the principle that 'children have a right to be listened to and for their views to be taken seriously about matters that affect them' (CWDC, 2008b). This is far from the Victorian notion that children should be 'seen and not heard'!

The United Nations Convention on the Rights of the Child and current UK legislation have played a significant role in providing the agenda for hearing the child's voice. Listening to babies, toddlers and young children is a skill – 'when Potter and Hodgeson (2007) analysed some tape-recorded conversations between nursery nurses and children, they found that staff began two thirds of the conversation. Such findings are worrying because we know that for children to become good communicators, it is very important that they have experiences of starting conversations' (Brock and Rankin, 2008: 50). We need to give toddlers and young children the opportunity to take the lead and use their own language rather than asking them to respond to us.

Your graduate studies will have informed your understanding about the importance of listening to children. Listening and paying attention to the ways that babies, toddlers and young children communicate informs our understanding about what is going on in their lives. Listening to a distressed baby crying informs us that the baby needs attention, be it for hunger, pain or a need of warmth and protection. Listening to a baby gurgling and

An EYP listening to children

babbling tells us that the baby is contented and happy. It is the EYP's role to encourage other practitioners, parents and carers to develop their personal skills in listening to the ways that babies, toddlers and young children express their feelings, concerns and interests. The benefits associated with listening to babies, toddlers and young children not only allows practitioners to assess the needs of the child and make personalized provision for them, it also makes the child feel valued, treasured and respected.

We all like to be listened to when we have got something to say and babies, toddlers and young children are no exception. 'Children of all ages, backgrounds and abilities are important, unique and worth listening to' (CWDC, 2008b: 50).

Listening carefully and valuing what babies, toddlers and young children have to say to us will enhance their feelings of self-worth and emotional well-being. At times, listening to babies and toddlers and young children may 'reveal situations of serious difficulty in the child's life of which the setting has been unaware. This includes disclosures of potential or actual harm' (CWDC, 2008b: 50).

You may have accessed training related to the Coram family's 'Listening to young children project' which was awarded the best educational project in the 2005 charity awards. It aims to support practitioners to become more responsive '… to the changes in children's lives, meeting their diverse needs and improving care and services' (Lancaster in Pugh and Duffy, 2006: 66). The project highlights a number of key factors that you may wish to take into consideration:

- Make time for children to be involved.
- Allocate space and time to document children's viewpoints.
- Offer a range of materials and opportunities for children to make choices.
- Allow children to choose whether they want to express their views or not.

For your EYPS assessments, you will need to demonstrate the ways in which you listen to and receive babies, toddlers and young children's views and take them seriously. You will also need to show how you respond to children, in a way that they can see their views have been listened to, even if it is not possible to do something about them.

Values and Attitudes

'Children flourish in an environment where they have positive role models and where adults treat children and each other with respect and courtesy' (CWDC, 2008b: 51).

Reflective Activity

Identify examples of the times that you have:

✓ praised examples of positive behaviour
✓ challenged unacceptable behaviour
✓ shown respect towards others
✓ shown regard for others' property and the environment
✓ shown punctuality, time management and reliability
✓ led and supported colleagues to behave in a manner that reflects the positive attitudes and values that they expect from children.

(Adapted from CWDC Guidance to the Standards (2008b.))

Look at the EYPS standard:

⇒ S28

It is true to say that not only children flourish in such an environment, and that the way that we treat our colleagues and other early years professionals should also reflect the professional values and attitudes that we expect babies, toddlers and young children to develop. Professional roles and responsibilities will be explored further in the next chapter (Chapter 8).

Key Points

✓ The government does not bring up children – parents do.
✓ It is important to find ways to sensitively acknowledge the demands made upon the modern-day family.

✓ 22 per cent of the leader's time may be spent in contact with parents and other professionals.

✓ Parents need to know what goes on day to day in the nursery so they don't get confused or panicked by what they hear in the media.

✓ Parents who are not involved in the early years sector cannot be expected to know as much as we do about child development and learning.

✓ Babies' learning is profoundly influenced by the interplay or 'proto-conversations' between themselves and their parents and carers.

✓ The United Nations Convention on the Rights of the Child and current UK legislation have played a significant role in providing the agenda for hearing the child's voice.

✓ Children of all ages, backgrounds and abilities are important, unique and worth listening to.

✓ Children flourish in an environment where they have positive role models and where adults treat children and each other with respect and courtesy.

Further Reading

Brock, A. and Rankin, C. (2008) *Communication, Language and Literacy from Birth to Five*. London: Sage.

Elfer, P., Goldschmied, E. and Selleck, D. (2003) *Key Persons in the Nursery: Building Relationships for Quality Provision*. London: David Fulton Publishers.

Whalley, M. (2007) *Involving Parents in their Children's* Learning. London: Paul Chapman Publishing.

Useful Websites

'All About Working with Parents' by the team at Pen Green Centre for Under-fives and Families, Corby, Northamptonshire:

✓ Rules of Engagement – The importance of working with parents
✓ Share Options – How to involve parents in their children's learning
✓ Close Encounters – Ways to build relationships with families
✓ Growing Together – Research and development work with parents and children under three.

See www.standards.dfes.gov.uk/eyfs/resources

(Extract from) 'All About ... Developing Positive Relations with Children' by Julian Grenier, Head of Kate Greenaway Nursery School, Islington, London – www.standards.dfes.gov.uk/eyfs

The Early Years Foundation Stage: Effective Practice: Key Person (2007) – www.standards.dfes.gov.uk/eyfs/resources

The United Nations Convention on the Rights of the Child (UNCRC) – www.unicef.org/crc/

CHAPTER 8

SUSTAINING TEAM WORK AND COLLABORATION AND PROFESSIONAL DEVELOPMENT NEEDS

This chapter is concerned with the EYP leader's role to develop and sustain effective ways to build a team culture of collaborative and cooperative working between colleagues in the early years context. The EYPS standards (S33–36) which fall under the umbrella of 'Team Work and Collaboration' are primarily concerned with the EYP's professional leadership, teamwork and collaboration – unlike the standards explored in the previous chapters, they do not relate to personal practice with young children. The EYPS 'Professional Development' standards (S37–39) also covered in this chapter and examines the EYP leader's ability to reflect on their own and their colleagues' practice and professional development needs, their ability to engage in innovative practice and their ability to bring about quality improvements, effect change and use literacy, numeracy and information and communication technology (ICT) to support children's learning and development, and their wider professional activities.

Innovative Leadership Striking a Balance (S39)

The EYP role is perceived as the linchpin for future effective early years provision: EYPs will have an important role in leading and supporting other staff by helping them to develop and improve their practice, establish and maintain positive relationships with and communicate and work in partnership with families and other professionals (CWDC, 2008b). To achieve this a balance needs to be struck between developing the leaders and the practitioners that deliver the early years foundation stage, so that they can in turn provide the opportunities for children to learn and develop and, ultimately, encourage them into lifelong learning.

By striking this balance, EYPs need to build a platform for long-term success by inspiring, supporting and guiding teams through complex situations to make joint decisions. As a result, leaders can both develop children and practitioners' learning while sustaining a culture of mutual respect and collaborative working.

This makes the EYP, by nature, talented and committed to the needs of both the practitioners and the children in their care. In this way, leaders in the early years sector are aligned with a vision to transform the delivery of the early years foundation stage.

To meet this goal, it is imperative for the EYP leader to develop and build a team of practitioners by instilling in them a sense of belonging and a sense of their own self-worth. In turn, leaders need to empower the practitioners around them to develop helpful attitudes and skills combined with the right level of knowledge, skills and understanding of the early years sector.

Through this process of empowering others, practitioners will support the vision set by the EYP by not only identifying the challenges that the whole team has to face, but by becoming involved in developing and initiating innovative solutions to bring about continuous improvements (S39). This relies on leaders in the sector having a strong sense of vision and underpinning values to support it, combined with a sense of enterprise and innovation, which they need the confidence and empowerment to deliver.

As such, early years leaders need to recognize their personal qualities as successful people and align their teams to provide children with rich and rewarding experiences and, in this way, feel part of the government's aspirational change process.

This questions, however, if it is just the research and government parameters that make practitioners inspirational early years leaders, or if legislation and guidelines provide the purpose, framework and tools for leading 'innovative' practice. Eden and Vangen (1994) would argue that 'those who think about the future, and whose thoughts have an impact on how that future will take shape, have a responsibility to examine the impact of the present logic of how organisations and managers operate. I believe that it is important to ask some 'whys' and not to continue to operate within the confines of the present conceptual order'.

Reflective Activity

Explain how you:

- ✓ continually review and improve practice and provision in order to achieve the best possible outcomes for children
- ✓ explore new ideas, products and developments in a creative and critical manner
- ✓ assess the benefits of implementing new ideas, products and developments and think carefully about whether or not they will achieve lasting change
- ✓ adapt practice if it can be shown that new ideas, products or developments will be of benefit and improve current practices and systems
- ✓ try out new ideas, products and developments and monitor and evaluate the effect
- ✓ accept when a new idea, product or development has not brought improvement and know how to modify an initial approach
- ✓ plan ways to involve those affected by change to gain acceptance
- ✓ make small and incremental changes and modifications of practice
- ✓ are open to innovative suggestions from others
- ✓ encourage colleagues to put forward their ideas and adapt their practice.

Look at the EYPS standard:
⇒ S39

The government's policy and aspiration to create a highly skilled workforce for the early years sector is based on research evidence. There are national workforce strategies to support and challenge practitioners to lead effective practice – for example, amongst other studies, the DfES funded the Longitudinal Study of Effective Provision of Pre-school Education (EPPE – Sylva et al., 2004), which demonstrates the 'positive effects of high quality provision on children's intellectual and social/behavioural developmental'.

Additionally, the ELEYS study recognized the challenge of developing leadership in the early years, highlighting the necessary qualities for the sector to:

- ✓ identify and articulate a collective vision
- ✓ ensure shared understandings, meanings and goals
- ✓ engage in effective communication
- ✓ encourage reflection
- ✓ develop a commitment to ongoing professional development
- ✓ monitor and assess practice

✓ distribute leadership
✓ build a learning community and team culture
✓ encourage and facilitate parent and community partnerships
✓ lead and manage, striking the balance to develop people and teams.

In March 2008, the Department for Children, Schools and Families (DCSF, 2007b) released *Children's plan – Building Brighter Futures: Next steps for the children's workforce.* This document sets out the actions the government is taking to build on existing investment, to further improve the skills and capacity of people who work with children and deliver the high-quality, personalized and integrated services which are set out in the Children's Plan. It also includes a chapter on Leadership and Management.

Multi-professional Team Working and Collaboration (S36)

The Children Act (2004) provided the legislative framework for Every Child Matters and includes the duty for interagency cooperation to improve children's well-being and the legal responsibility of all agencies to work together to safeguard children and promote their welfare. This approach requires professionals to work together and share information so that children are protected from harm and neglect and achieve better outcomes. Sadly, this was as a consequence of the tragic death of Victoria Climbié, the young girl who was horrifically abused and tortured, and eventually killed by her great aunt and the man with whom she lived. The government green paper (DfES, 2003b) was published alongside the formal response to the report into the death of Victoria Climbié led by Lord Laming during 2003. There was a wide consultation with people working in children's services, and with parents, children and young people. Following the consultation, the government published *Every Child Matters: Next Steps* (DfES, 2004e) and passed the Children Act (2004), providing the legislative context for developing more effective and accessible services focused around the needs of children, young people and families. The setting up of children's trusts is a further development of Lord Laming's report of the inquiry into the death of Victoria Climbié: 'Children's trusts are intended to encourage collaborative and coordinated working across agencies. They aim to engage education, health and social care agencies and service users, along with other partners such as Sure Start ...' (DfES, 2005).

The *Building Brighter Futures: Next steps for the children's workforce* (DCSF, 2007b) document sets out actions to build on the existing investment made and further improve the skills and capacity of professionals who work with children.

EYP candidates from a children's centre, daycare setting, local authority advisory service and childminding network working collaboratively

The public document 'Values for Integrated Working with Children and Young People' (released for circulation in March 2008 by the GTC, NMC and GSCC) suggests that:

✓ Children's practitioners value the contribution that a range of colleagues make to children and young people's lives, and they form effective relationships across the children's workforce.
✓ Their integrated practice is based on a willingness to bring their own expertise to bear on the pursuit of shared goals, and a respect for the expertise of others.
✓ Practitioners recognize that children, young people, families and colleagues value transparency and reliability, and strive to make sure that processes, roles, goals and resources are clear.
✓ Practitioners involved in integrated work recognize the need to be clear about lines of communication, management and accountability as these may be more complex than in their specialist setting.
✓ They uphold the standards and values of their own professions in their interprofessional work.
✓ They understand that sharing responsibility for children's outcomes does not mean acting beyond their competence or responsibilities.
✓ They are committed to taking action if safety or standards are compromised, whether that means alerting their own manager/employer or another appropriate authority.

✓ Children's practitioners understand that the knowledge, understanding and skills-integrated work may differ from those in their own specialism.

✓ They are committed to reflecting on and improving their interprofessional practice, and to engaging with relevant research and other evidence.

Team working and collaboration is multifaceted – it may involve EYPs working in a multi-agency context, which potentially can range from a group of practitioners deciding to work informally together to support a child or family, right through to a large-scale venture like a new service coming together under the umbrella of a Sure Start Children's Centre. Early years teams work in a variety of settings, for example PVI pre-schools, Children's Centres, the advisory services and childminding. Within those settings, there are varying types of teams – the baby room team, the toddler room team, the rising five or plus four team. Within the advisory services, there are Early Years Advisory teachers, Special Educational Needs teams, Additional Education Needs teams and learning consultants to name but a few. Childminders have their own network teams, while FE college lecturers may belong to a health team, an education team or the social care team. Sure Start Children's Centres offer the opportunity to belong to a range of multidisciplinary teams. In some private settings, teams have evolved mainly by parents and friendship groups starting up their own provision.

 Reflective Activity

Identify a time that you worked collaboratively or in partnership on an early years initiative, for example:

✓ running and contributing to workshops
✓ organizing meetings with colleagues or professionals
✓ leading a discussion about ways of improving provision and practice
✓ planning and delegating work to colleagues who you supervise
✓ giving advice and support to a colleague
✓ resolving areas of potential or actual conflict
✓ offering or seeking the knowledge and skills and advice of another professional.

(Adapted from CWDC Guidance to the Standards (2008b)).

Look at the EYPS standard:

⇒ S33

The concept of team working for an EYP has many variables, for example you may be part of one team but work on occasions with another team, and you may be part of a team that has been pulled together for a short activity or a project. Handy (1999: 150) provides a description of team working: 'They vary from the formal – a work group, a project team, a committee, a board – to the informal – the ad hoc meeting or discussion, the luncheon group, the clique, the cabal. They are permanent or temporary. They are liked by their members or regarded as a waste of time. They can be a most effective device for blocking and obstructing a new idea, or the best way of putting them into practice'.

I believe that the metaphor of 'kaleidoscope' best describes the interrelationships, people joining teams, teams being set up and teams being disbanded, teams being added to or downsized, EYPs being a leader in one and participant in another. In essence, 'most organisations rely on teams and team work to achieve their goals and objectives' (McCall and Lawler, 2000: 32).

Through your graduate studies, you may have become familiar with theories related to the roles needed within a team for it to work effectively. These include an ideas person, implementor, coordinator, finisher, specialist, evaluator, and team worker. Belbin (1981) offers 'Team Theory' which provides an insight into internal group relationships and the roles required for a team or group to work effectively. In comparison, Huczynski and Buchanan (1991) offer functions performed by teams as task roles and maintenance roles. Task roles include initiator, information and opinion seekers, evaluator, decision maker and diagnoser whilst maintenance roles include compromiser, clarifier, encourager, standards setter and pace keeper.

As EYPS standard 33 asks you to demonstrate the ways in which you have 'established and sustained a culture of collaborative and cooperative working between colleagues' (CWOC, 2008b), you may wish to consider the purpose and function of any teams that you influence and identify the roles of individuals working in those teams (S34).

The behaviours of the teams that you influence will be of significance to the way in which you have developed a 'culture of collaborative and cooperative working'. Handy (1976) in Huczynski and Buchanan (1991: 198) believes that when individuals decide about behaviour in a group, they are concerned with the three issues presented in the point for reflection on p. 35.

Handy's (1976) group behaviour characteristics imply that in order for EYPs to establish and sustain a culture of effective team work and collaboration, they will need to have strategies worked out in advance, be mentally prepared, have questions and answers in place and, at the same time, be open to suggestions. Figure 8.1, adapted from CWDC *Guidance to the Standards* (2008b) and the public document 'Values for Integrated Working with Children and Young People' (released for circulation in March 2008), identifies the key elements of effective team work and collaboration.

Point for Reflection

Group Behaviour:

Identity

'Who am I in this group? What is my occupational role? What are the role expectations of me?'

Power

'Who has the power? What kind of power is it? Do I want to change the influence pattern?'
'What are my needs and objectives? Are they in line with this group? What do I do about them if they are not?'
(Adapted from Handy (1976) in Huczynski and Buchanan (1991: 198))

Look at the EYPS standard:

⇒ S34

Belbin's (1981) research suggests that it is dangerous to combine too many of the same type of team roles together. He goes as far as to say that the most ill-fated teams can be the ones that are exclusively composed of very clever people, referring to this as the 'Apollo Syndrome'. There are nine team roles in Belbin's model, and individuals may act as a Plant at the beginning of a project but as a Specialist later on, etc. This suggests that a team of Plants might be very creative but unlikely to implement their ideas; conversely, a team of Implementers might be very practical but would lack the creativity to be innovative. Belbin's theory would therefore suggest that in building effective teams, EYPs need to be aware that colleagues may take on different team role characteristics at different times of an activity or project, or indeed you may yourself.

The way that you sustain a culture of collaborative working when a new member joins the team should be reflected upon. Schein (1992) cited by Hatch (2000: 217) suggests that 'when new members of the group are brought into a culture they are either selected on the basis of the match between their values and those of the culture or they are socialized to accept cultural values'. This implies that you will use your skills (within the confines of British employment law of course) to recruit and induct new members to the ways of working in your setting, group or team, in order to sustain the status quo.

Point for Reflection

The *Children's Plan – Building Brighter Futures* (DCSF, 2007b) advocates that the qualities of an effective leader of integrated services are the ability to:

- ✓ provide a commitment to quality
- ✓ inspire others through personal enthusiasm
- ✓ encourage, mobilize, connect and support others
- ✓ build, maintain and nurture close reciprocal relationships
- ✓ recognize the importance and mutual benefits of networking
- ✓ secure the trust of others
- ✓ value the contributions and views of others
- ✓ safeguard and promote the welfare of others
- ✓ be creative and communicative
- ✓ display resilience and tenacity in the face of difficulties and challenge
- ✓ reflect on personal performance.

Look at the EYPS standard:

⇒ S36

As well as possessing such qualities, it is important to remind ourselves that the colleagues we are encouraging to work collaboratively and cooperatively have psychological needs of their own. We all need to have a sense of recognition, security and belonging. 'We need a human side to leadership and leaders who can engage authentically, both emotionally and intellectually. We need leaders who fundamentally realise the need to engage, interact and connect with each other and ultimately to recognise the common, frail and ultimately vulnerable humanity that we all share' (Vagers (2008) article on the EYPS forum website, April 2008). Benson in Bruce (2006: 287) supports the notion that the concept of emotional intelligence is vital to team working. Figure 8.1, p. 138 offers a model for leading team work and collaboration that needs to be considered very carefully, as failure in any one of the key areas has the potential to have a detrimental effect on the other two.

Leadership

To put the role of the EYP leader into an early years context, the traditional nursery rhyme 'I'm following my leader, my leader, my leader, I'm following my leader' springs to my mind. I also use the story of the 'enormous turnip' in my training to illustrate how a team relies not only on the strength of the leader but also the followers: 'Leadership is about motivating others to followship' (Law and Glover, 2000 in Rodd, 2006).

Written Activity

Review Jillian Rodd's 'Stages of Team Development' (2006: 152–60) below and identify how they compare to your experiences of team working:

Stage 1: Connecting – Getting the team together
Stage 2: Confronting conflict in the team
Stage 3: Cooperating as a team
Stage 4: Collaborating as an effective team
Stage 5: Closure

Look at the EYPS standards:

⇒ S33, S34, S36

In your EYPS assessments, you will need to find ways to show your assessor how you inspire 'followers', and how you meet their needs and what resources you make available.

Leading and developing teams is not an easy task – it takes time, effort and intuition. In my experience, you need to gain credibility, to be a cheer leader and remain calm and composed, or to use a metaphor, 'like a swan calm and serene on the top and paddling like mad underneath!'. Rodd (2006: 152) identifies that teams need to be led from 'birth to maturity'. Your graduate studies may have informed you of the 'forming, storming, norming, performing and adjourning' (Curren, 1998 in Rodd, 2006: 153) phases of team development.

In my personal experience, the 'storming' stage of a team's development is best 'nipped in the bud', as, if conflict situations are not dealt with immediately, *micro* political forces have the potential to become *macro* political forces.

Rodd (2006: 112) believes that '… conflict experience in early years settings may be related to the style of leadership displayed'. While it is widely acknowledged that there are many contemporary theories on leadership styles that relate to corporate organizations, schools and other fields, the literature reviewed suggests that the traditional approaches to leadership do not readily translate to EYP leaders. Kagen in Rodd (2006: 10) 'identifies the shortcomings of three traditional approaches to understanding leadership: personal characteristics and traits; style behaviour and strategies; and the nature of the task and work culture'. Arguably, Harris (2007: 173) believes that 'the old managerial list models of leadership are no longer suited to an age that is fast paced, technologically driven and globally focused. We are using theories and models of leadership that simply do not suit the contemporary educational landscape'. So until such time that a model for Early Years Leadership is in circulation, we can only interpret the old management list of models into new ways of thinking.

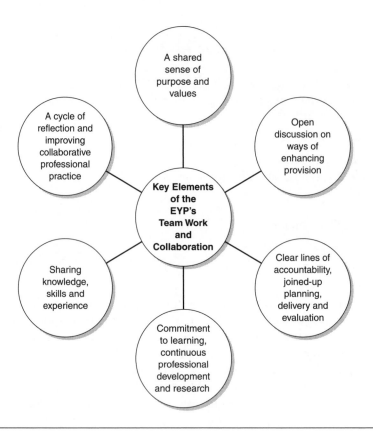

Figure 8.1   *Key elements of teamwork and collaboration*

Adapted from CWDC *Guidance to the Standards* (2008b) and the public document 'Values for Integrated Working with Children and Young People' (Released for circulation March 2008)

Goleman et al. (2002) believe that good leaders are effective because they create resonance. Resonance comes from the Latin word *resonare*, meaning to 'resound'. For EYP leadership, this means using a facilitative approach rather than an authoritative approach. Goleman et al. (2002) offer the 'six ways of leading to six leadership styles' model. Simplistically put, the model gives EYP leaders the opportunity to consider switching between leadership styles by attuning themselves to other people's feelings and finding ways to support them to become emotionally secure. In the early years, 'leadership is exercised in a climate of reciprocal relationships where the leader seeks to act *with* others rather than assert power *over* others' (Rodd, 2006: 33). Thus, Goleman's theory would suggest that this can be done by 'resonating' a personal vision, values and direction with emotional intelligence. This relates nicely to the 'leadership point of view' activity presented in Chapter 2, p. 36.

Goleman's 'resonance-building' approach (Goleman et al., 2002) sits nicely alongside the contingency approach to leadership. They are both based on the idea that

Table 8.1   *Warren Bennis – Four rules of leadership*

Leaders:

- provide direction and meaning and a sense of purpose
- generate and sustain trust, creating authentic relationships
- display a bias towards action, risk taking and curiosity
- are purveyors of hope, optimism and a psychological resilience that expects success.

Source: Kennedy, 1998: 30

there is no one best way to lead and that to be effective, your style must be tailored to the particular task or situation that you are challenged by. Adair's (1983) 'Action Centered Leadership (ACL)' model fits neatly into a facilitative style of leadership and shows the interconnectivity between the roles of leading the task, team and situation.

One of the most significant features of an EYP's role is to develop people within the multi complex nature of the EYFS, the environment and more importantly the children and families that you are accountable to.

Leadership and Motivation

As discussed earlier in this chapter the EYPS standards 33–36 are concerned with the role of the EYPs' professional leadership, their support to their colleagues and their ability to foster teamwork and collaboration – they do not pertain to managerial responsibilities, '… which fall outside the remit of the Standards for EYPS' (CWDC, 2008b). Many authorities have debated the difference between leadership and management in the early years. I tend to support the notion of Law and Glover (Rodd, 2006: 23) that 'the knowledge, abilities and skills of management and leadership are different but overlapping'.

Bennis (in Kennedy, 1998: 29) suggests that:

Managers do things right,
Leaders do the right thing.

As also mentioned earlier in the book, there is not a definitive model for the Early Years Leader. 'We are seeking to define a new model or paradigm of leadership which best fits Early Years Professional Status…' (Whalley et al., 2008). However, in the absence of such a model, you may wish to consider Warren Bennis's four rules of leadership (Kennedy, 1998: 30) illustrated in Table 8.1. As Whalley et al. (2008: 9) point out, 'The model of leadership practice for EYPS is one that must fit across all types of early years settings and sit equally comfortably in a home setting, a voluntary pre-school in a small village hall, a private nursery or a large children's centre'.

Peters and Waterman (1982) advocate that leadership and motivation are considered to be two of the most critical factors in achieving excellence. Through your EYP's graduate studies, you may have come across theories of motivating people. Adair (in Kennedy, 1984: 4) suggests a 'fifty-fifty rule' for motivating individuals, meaning that motivation is an innate feature of individual behaviour, believing that '… half an individual's motivation comes from within himself or herself, the other half from external factors, including leadership'. If this is the case, then the metaphor 'Physician heal thyself' (Bush and Middlewood, 1997: 25) suggests that EYPs must go through a self-analysis process to identify their own strengths, weaknesses and expectations in order to engage effectively with and motivate others to want to work collaboratively. Moyles (2006) offers a tool for leaders to evaluate their own effectiveness in the 'Effective Leadership and Management Scheme – Early Years' by using the metaphor of a tree where EYPs can explore their professional attributes, personal characteristics and attitudes. Goleman (1999: 31) in Bruce (2006: 287) defines this self-analysis as '… emotional intelligence (EQ): the capacity for recognizing our own feelings and those of others for motivating ourselves and for managing emotions well in ourselves and in our relationships'. Goleman believes that EQ in the early years is more important than the level of IQ!

Looking after Professional Development Needs (S38)

Keeping abreast of the rapidly changing developments in the early years sector relies on the EYP leaders' commitment to continuous professional development both for themselves and their colleagues. EYPS standard 38 asks you to reflect on, and evaluate the impact of, your own practice on children's learning and development, and encourage colleagues to do likewise. EYPs create the time in which to reflect upon what they are doing, either individually or with colleagues, to assess their performance. Identify gaps in their knowledge and/or its practical application, and take steps to seek continuous professional development.

'This includes the personal study of current research and other sources of effective practice, and/or attendance at professional development events. It may involve observing the practice of colleagues in their own or other settings, in order to be able to make comparisons and gain new ideas, or arranging shadowing or mentoring opportunities' (CWDC, 2008b: 73). As a LA advisory teacher, it was my role to provide information and training about new developments and approaches, to early years practitioners for example healthy eating initiatives, the Reggio Emillio approach and Leuven scales of well-being and involvement.

Reflective Activity

Provide examples of times that you have:

✓ reflected upon and evaluated the effectiveness of your practice
✓ modified and adapted your approach where necessary

✓ drawn on research outcomes and other sources of effective practice as a way of informing and improving your own and your colleagues' practice
✓ identified your own need for additional professional development and supported colleagues to do likewise
✓ identified where to gain access to sources of continuing professional development and support for yourself and, where appropriate, for your colleagues.

(Adapted from CWDC Guidance to the Standards (2008b))

Look at the EYPS standard:

⇒ S38

Twenty-first Century Technologies

Reflect back to the start of this millennium and consider the technological changes and challenges you have mastered since then. I know that the wealth of changes that I have had to respond to associated with the government ECM agenda (discussed in the first chapter) have been truly amazing. The introduction of EYPS has given me the opportunity to lead a project that I am 100 per cent signed up for; I am delighted that we now have a nationally recognized status and that people are talking about EYPS as the gold standard to aspire to. EYPS has given me the opportunity to extend my networking with early years colleagues from across the country and share expertise and experience.

Technology has also played a big role in my life – at the click of a mouse, I can now access government documents and policies, engage in online debates, send information to my colleagues, undertake online mentoring, send minutes and agendas to my colleagues. I am always truly inspired when I see how technology has transformed early years settings. I recently visited one setting that uses digital cameras as part of their child observations; another setting shows these photographs at the start and end of each session so that the parents/carers can see the activities that their children have been engaging in. Word processors have made it easier to collate information, write up plans and record children's assessments. Labelling on displays is much clearer when word-processed and the comic sans font is easy for a child to recognize. Not wanting to age myself but I can remember the days when I would draw lines to get my letter spacing perfect! I have also seen some great examples of newsletters, notices and booklets produced for parents – this would not have been possible without photocopiers, scanners and printers.

Excel spreadsheets and calculators help practitioners to work out staff and children ratios. Budgets for children's healthy meals, snacks and drinks have to be managed and, in many PVI settings, so do staff salaries and room hire costs. The introduction of

An EYP childminder candidate supporting an ICT activity with a child

ICT has been a challenge to many early years settings. Many PVI settings operate from village, church or community halls, and childminders from their own homes. Training has been very scarce and so have the resources. Many early years professionals have taken it upon themselves to become computer literate, and the sector has relied on the good will of professionals to use their personal computers and laptops.

Reflective Activity

Reflect on the ways that you use your skills in literacy, numeracy and ICT to:

✓ support your wider professional activities
✓ lead and support your colleagues to develop and apply their skills in literacy, numeracy and ICT.

Literacy	Numeracy	ICT

(Adapted from CWDC Guidance to the Standards (2008b))

Look at the EYPS standard:

⇒ S37

As an EYP you will be looking for innovative ways to embrace technology. Today's children are primates of the technological age – they do not know any difference as they are born into a world of technological wonders and need enabling adults to extend their learning and development more than ever before. The changes that technology brought about in the earlier part of the twentieth century have now been accelerated into the twenty-first century. Nutbrown (2006) believes that radical changes have made an impact on almost every aspect of life in many parts of the world, and the early years in Britain is no exception. 'These changes have provided equipment for work and leisure for adults and the education and play of young children which has surpassed any possible imagining. Literacy, for example, is no longer about putting a pen to paper but increasingly about putting fingers to a keyboard, and reading material is not only available in a static printed form but also in fluid forms on computer and television screens – leading to new definitions of literacy' (Barton and Hamilton, 1998). Indeed, the opening ceremony of the Olympics 2008 held in Beijing featured time-honoured Chinese drummers beating digitally controlled sound to light drums in a spectacular sequence and was viewed all over the world on satellite television.

Reflective Activity

Reflect on the ways that you engage the support of others to make provision for children's learning and development needs in literacy, numeracy and ICT, for example in:

✓ contributing to each of the six areas of learning and development in the EYFS
✓ the development of children's language and communication skills
✓ the development of children's shape, pattern and number skills
✓ the development of children's emotional and social skills
✓ the development of children's everyday problem solving, reasoning and numeracy skills
✓ the provision of creative and challenging activities and resources, both in spoken and written language
✓ dealing with children who have learning difficulties or disabilities, additional needs, or those for whom English is not their first language
✓ communication for young children's well-being, learning and development
✓ opportunities for children to become familiar with ICT, for example personal computers and software, toys that can be programmed, whiteboards, digital cameras and video-recorders.

Literacy	Numeracy	ICT

(Adapted from CWDC Guidance to the Standards (2008b)).

Look at the EYPS standard:

⇒ S37

Influencing Policies and Practices (S35)

Another feature of the EYP leader is the expert knowledge and understanding of the current policies and practices of the setting. Policies and procedures are of paramount importance in the setting, as they not only provide a framework for the working practices that impact on the safeguarding, Health and Safety, well-being, learning and development of the babies, toddlers and young children, but they also influence the behaviours and the way in which colleagues conduct themselves. Well-written and up-to-date policies and procedures can support your explanation of the principles and values that inform and steer the early years provision, and at the same time show how they comply with the Learning and Development requirements and the Welfare Requirements associated with the EYFS (DCSF, 2008b: 66). CWDC (2008b) suggest that policy documents should '... incorporate a wide spectrum of activities, such as aimed at implementing the EYFS and achieving the five ECM outcomes, and include:

- the assessment of children's progress
- equality and inclusion
- health and safety
- child protection and safeguarding
- relationships with children and parents/carers.'

Ebbeck and Waniganayake's 'typology of administration management and leadership' in Rodd (2006: 57–8) suggests that training, design and direct policy development are part of the roles and responsibilities of a leader and that policy formation is concerned with the leader's ability to facilitate leadership skills related to macro-level engagement, both inside and outside the centre, which are primarily concerned with the future.

Reflective Activity

Consider how you:

- ✓ influence and shape the policies and practices of the setting
- ✓ analyse the current effectiveness of the policies and practice in your setting
- ✓ apply your knowledge of best practice to the policies and procedures of the setting
- ✓ lead colleagues in a collective process of continuous review of existing policy and practice
- ✓ lead colleagues in policy making
- ✓ lead colleagues in the implementation of new policies
- ✓ involve parents and children in policy making.

(Adapted from CWDC Guidance to the Standards (2008b))

Look at the EYPs Standard:

⇒ SS35

Key Points

✓ Early years team work and collaboration rely not only on the strength of EYP leaders but also the followers.

✓ Early years teams need to be led from 'birth to maturity'.

✓ It is important to deal with conflict situations, as *micro* political forces have the potential to become *macro* political forces.

✓ Managers *do things right*; Leaders *do the right thing*.

✓ EYP leaders need to communicate expectation, optimism and emotional resilience.

✓ Fifty per cent of motivation comes from the individual, the other fifty per cent from the leader.

✓ Today's children are primates of the technological age, so find innovative ways to lead technologically driven practice.

✓ EYP leaders can influence and innovate team working through policies and procedures.

Further Reading

Children's Workforce Development Council (CWDC) (2007) *Championing children.* Leeds: CWDC.

Goleman, D., Boyatzis, R. and McKee, A. (2002) *Primal Leadership: Realizing the Power of Emotional Intelligence.* Harvard: Harvard Business School Press.

Rodd, J. (2006) *Leadership in Early Childhood*, 3rd edition. Maidenhead: Open University Press.

Useful Websites

Businessballs: Free career help, business training, organizational development, innovative ideas, materials, exercises, tools and templates – www.businessballs.net/

Department for Children, Schools and Families (DCSF, 2008): *Building Brighter Futures: Next Steps for the Children's Workforce* – publications.everychildmatters.gov.uk – reference 00292–2008.

Muijs, D., Aubrey, C., Harris, A. and Briggs, M. (2004) 'How do they manage? A review of the research in Early Childhood', *Journal of Early Childhood Research*, 2: 157. Available at: ecr.sagepub.com/cgi/content/abstract/2/2/157

CHAPTER 9

GOING THROUGH THE GATEWAY

This chapter will be given to exploring the first stage of the EYPS assessment process, the 'Gateway Review of Skills' and ways in which practitioners aiming to gain EYPS can demonstrate the leadership characteristics required in the assessment. Chapter 10 will examine the requirement for the final stages of assessment – the Written Tasks and the Setting Visit. This chapter will make links with Chapter 2, with reference to the EYPS validation process which is the same for each of the four EYPS pathways. Links will be made to the theory and reflective tasks in relation to the EYPS standards (CWDC, 2008b) discussed in Chapters 3 to 8. This chapter will provide the opportunity for reflective thinking in relation to the characteristics required of the practitioners to lead, model and support other staff in helping them to bring about change, improve early years practice, establish and maintain positive relationships with children and develop the EYP's abilities to communicate and work in partnership with families, carers and other professionals.

The EYPS Assessment Process

Regardless of which EYPS pathway you are undertaking, you will undergo the same assessment process within the last four months of your programme. Chapter 1 provided you with an overview of the EYPS assessment process and of how the EYPS standards are organized. Your personal EYPS assessment process will comprise of the following three activities:

1. **The Gateway Review of Skills**

   Your training provider will invite you to attend a half-day assessment to review your understanding of the EYPS standards and assess your skills through a number of exercises together with a small number of other EYPS candidates.

2. **A Set of Written Tasks**

   You will need to write and submit a number of reflective accounts to your training provider by a set deadline. These must show how your knowledge and understanding of the early years sector underpin aspects of your personal practice and leadership and support of others against the 39 EYPS standards and across the full age range (0–5 years). You will need to produce a small file of documentary evidence to support these tasks for your assessor to review when they visit your setting.

3. **The Setting Visit**

   In this final stage of your assessment, an assessor will visit you in your work place or, if you are not normally based in a setting, a setting that you have identified. During the visit, your assessor will corroborate what you have said in your written tasks by conducting a series of interviews with yourself and three nominated witnesses, reviewing your small file of documentary evidence and undertaking a tour of your setting.

In the Gateway Review of Skills assessment, you will only need to show that you understand the content and purpose of the EYPS standards and the way that you are working towards them. As you progress to the two final stages of your assessments, you will need to demonstrate how you meet the CWDC 39 professional EYPS standards in your practice with children from birth to five years. 'The Standards are outcome statements that describe what Early Years Professionals need to know, understand and be able to do, and apply to practice with children from birth to the end of the EYFS: that is, babies, toddlers and young children' (CWDC, 2008b: 7).

Your attendance at EYPS training sessions, your review of course work materials, the CWDC *Candidate Handbook* (2008a), the CWDC *Guidance to the Standards* (2008b) and your graduate studies and research will inform your understanding of the CWDC EYPS standards which are organized into the following six groups:

✓ Knowledge and understanding (covered in Chapters 3 to 8)
✓ Effective practice (covered in Chapters 4 to 6)
✓ Relationships with children (covered in Chapter 7)
✓ Communicating and working in partnership with families and carers (covered in Chapter 7)

✓ Team work and collaboration (covered in Chapter 8)
✓ Professional development.

Remember that the standards set out what you need to meet in order to gain the EYP status.

Point for Reflection

Remember that no hierarchy is implied by the order in which the standards are presented. Although each standard is described discretely, there are interrelationships, both within each group of standards and between the groups of standards. The knowledge and understanding outlined in the first six standards will inform all aspects of your effective practice as discussed in Chapter 4.

(Adapted from the CWDC Candidate Handbook (2008a))

The evidence that you provide to support your claim for the standards and any decisions that you refer to in your assessments must reflect 'graduate-ness'. This means providing well-informed explanations about your practice based on your knowledge of relevant theories, research, government policies, guidance and the Early Years Foundation Stage DCSF (2008a: 2) You will need to firstly, show how you react to changes and respond flexibly to children's needs and interests and secondly, how you review, analyse and evaluate your own and other colleagues practice and how you use this information to assess whether a difference is being made to the well-being, learning and development of the children.

In summary, whatever your role and wherever you work, your EYPS assessments will need to show:

✓ the context within which you work
✓ your personal relevant experience of leading, modelling and supporting early years practice

and the way that you:

✓ lead and support your colleagues to make a positive impact on children's well-being, learning and development across the full age range (0–5 years)
✓ lead change through innovative practice to improve outcomes for babies, toddlers and young children
✓ possess a commitment to delivering high-quality early years provision.

Don't use the 'I' Word

Your assessments are all about you, your practice, your leadership and your support of others. Many of my EYPS candidates find it difficult to use the 'I' word when communicating either verbally or in writing. It is very important to state 'I' not 'we'. They often describe situations or events by saying 'we organized'. They often use the old adage, quite correctly, that 'there is no I in TEAM' and that much of their practice relies on team working. My response to this has always been to agree that there is not an 'I' in team, however there is a 'me' and the EYPS assessment process is all about the way that this 'me' does things. The use of the 'I' pronoun at the beginning of a statement or sentence in contrast to 'we, they or some of us' allows you to appropriately express your professional competencies and thus prevent ambiguity about your leadership capabilities.

Emotional Intelligence

As mentioned in Chapter 8, CWDC (2008b) define the support given by the EYP leaders as independent of their position in their setting, network or service and where they do not have to be the setting owner or manger. It has also been recognized throughout this book that there is a wide diversity of roles within the early years PVI sector, for example you may work as a childminder, or within a pre-school or nursery, in a Sure Start Children's Centre, a full daycare setting, as a Local Authority advisory teacher or as a Further Education tutor. Wherever you work or whatever your job role the EYPS assessment process will be the same regardless of your background and the setting or service that you work in. The assessment process that you undertake will be the same for you as it will be for everyone else; rest assured that this will ensure that your assessment process will be robust and nationally consistent (CWDC, 2008b).

I have supported a number of EYPS candidates who do not hold senior positions in their settings to identify ways of evidencing their leadership and support of others. While many have been employed in response to the government's agenda to have a graduate-led workforce, they have had to show high levels of respect and regard to lesser qualified colleagues who have been in post as supervisors, room leaders' deputies and managers for lengthy periods of time. In some instances, it has been challenging for these candidates to gain the support and recognition of these colleagues who often espouse the old chestnut: 'we have been doing it this way for x amount of years and don't see why we should change!' These candidates have shown me how they have worked skilfully with their colleagues by developing their ability to use 'emotional intelligence' as a way of gaining credibility and influencing practice. Confident and enthusiastic leaders are those '… who communicate through beliefs, actions and words that they have a strong sense of self, and are committed to making an impact on the lives of children and adults they interact with, [and who] attract followers who are willing to be guided in the direction taken by the leader' (Rodd, 2006: 66).

Points for Reflection

Read the copy below of an email between an EYPS candidate and their mentor:

Hi X,

Have you considered demonstrating your leadership within the context of how you use 'emotional intelligence' to tap into your colleague's reluctance to take on board new ideas in your setting?

For example, consider:

(a) times when you have consistently modelled good practice or offered new ways of working to your colleagues in a manner that has got them thinking and wanting to give it a go
(b) times that you have used 'emotional intelligence' to overcome feelings of being dejected because your idea or way of working was not being taken seriously.

Very often, our emotions can impede the way we react intelligently to a situation, however in your assessments you must show the way that you react intelligently to these situations and seek a solution-focused approach.

I hope that this helps, and please get back to me with your thoughts.

Denise

The Gateway Review of Skills

This review comprises four exercises and a written reflection which have been designed to replicate similar ones used within education, health and the private sector to assess the professional competencies of their leaders. The activities that you will engage in consist of:

- a personal interview
- a written exercise
- a group exercise
- an interview with an actor
- a written reflection.

The assessment process is designed to do two things: firstly, to check your understanding of the EYPS standards and, secondly, to assess your ability against the three generic skills listed in Table 2.2, deemed necessary to work at the level required of an EYP and for meeting the EYPS standards.

Personal Interview

To organize yourself for the Gateway Review, you will attend some preparation days with your training provider. These days will help you examine the nature and scope of the EYPS standards and access how comfortable you feel about meeting each one. Before the Gateway Review, you will need to submit an analysis of each group of standards to your training provider. In your analysis, you will indicate which standards you will find easy to meet and why, and which ones you feel that you will need to undertake further research or attend training for, in order to prepare yourself for the final stages of your assessment process, the Written Tasks and the Setting Visit.

 Points for Reflection

To prepare yourself for any discussion that you may have with your Personal Interview Gateway Review assessor, rehearse your responses to the following questions:

1. Which standards am I most confident about and why?
2. Which standards am I least confident about and why?
3. What background research, government policies, documents or frameworks do I need to consult to inform my knowledge of the standards that I am not feeling very confident about?
4. What training do I need to access, where and when is it taking place and what arrangements do I need to make?
5. What work experience do I need to organize, and what will be the focus of this?

Your training provider will arrange for a copy of your Standards Review analysis to be sent to your Gateway Review assessor who will scrutinize it before your review takes place and use it to inform the basis of the Personal Interview. Try to spend some time preparing for your personal interview and your interview with the actor: control your breathing, eat well before the processes, have some water to drink nearby, pause before answering questions, don't be frightened to ask for something to be clarified and try not to talk too much and go off at a tangent.

Table 9.1   *Reflections from EYPS candidates on the Gateway Review of Skills*

Personal Interview

'The personal interview was interesting and not daunting as I expected, more relaxed'
'My verbal communication skills are stronger than I previously thought'
'It was useful to reflect on my experience against the standards'
'I had to speak slowly so that my assessor could write things down, this meant holding on to my thoughts'
'It helped me to clarify my thinking'

During your Personal Interview, your assessor will discuss your understanding of the standards and the level at which you have been working in your recent and present roles. During your interview, your assessor will be writing everything down as near as word verbatim as possible, so aim to give clear explanations, and don't go off at a tangent and speak at a reasonable pace. Remember that your assessor will be making a judgement about the way that you communicate (see point 3 in Table 2.2, p. 27).

Written Exercise

The Written Exercise, like the other three Gateway Review exercises, is designed to assess your ability against the three generic skills illustrated in Table 2.2, p. 27. However, if the exercise is time-pressured – you will be asked to respond to five or six scenarios that mirror the type of things that you may have encountered in your setting, network or service.

Point for Reflection

Written Exercise

'This exercise will consist of five or six items. These might be 'post-it' notes, reported telephone conversations, a letter from a parent/carer or other miscellaneous items that you might have to tackle in the course of your normal working week. You will not usually have to respond directly to each but rather state what you would do, when you would do so and by what means. You will also be asked to highlight any issues that need to be considered.'

CWDC *Candidate Handbook* (2008a: 7)

In making your responses, you will need to demonstrate your ability to think on your feet and make informed decisions both efficiently and effectively. Rodd (2006: 253–57)

Table 9.2 *Reflections from EYPS candidates on the Gateway Review of Skills*

Written Exercise

'I found the writing task easiest, as I feel more comfortable writing than talking'
'I would normally spend more time reflecting on how to respond to such issues'
'You wouldn't normally have to deal with so many issues in such a short space of time'
'I had to think and write my answers very quickly'

discusses the fact that in the early years, decisions are often made quickly without discussion or consultation with others. In order to make decisions that protect children's rights and act in everyone's best interests, they should be informed by a 'code of ethics'. In all aspects of your work, it is much easier to act with professional integrity and make moral judgements based on personal values and belief systems. 'Ethical leadership is a process of working with people to achieve specific goals, and is founded on trust, values, respect, communication, collaboration and empowerment' (Rodd, 2006: 257).

The types of decisions that you have to make in your daily practice can be anything, ranging from a parental complaint to an unexpected event like having to evacuate the children from an area of the setting due to a health and safety issue.

During the 'Written Exercise', you will need to demonstrate a good working knowledge of national and local policies, procedures and frameworks and the EYFS (2008). Remember that your assessor will be making a judgement against the three generic skills illustrated in Table 2.2, p. 27. You may wish to consider ways to:

✓ think beyond the immediate issue presented in the written item and avoid a 'quick fix' solution (Table 2.2, point 1)
✓ concentrate on what the most important issue is in each written item (Table 2.2, point 1)
✓ make an appropriate decision for each of the written items using the information presented (Table 2.2, point 1)
✓ make a record of any additional information you would like to see and identify how to obtain it (Table 2.2, point 1)
✓ base any decisions that you record on agreed principles, the code of ethics and setting policies (Table 2.2, point 1)
✓ recognize and develop the potential of others (Table 2.2, point 2)
✓ propose clear strategies to improve the situation (Table 2.2, point 2)
✓ identify issues of poor practice and ways of supporting and developing colleagues (Table 2.2, point 2)
✓ listen to others' concerns in the written item and make an appropriate response (Table 2.2, point 3)
✓ show respect for others in a sensitive manner (Table 2.2, point 3)
✓ communicate clearly in writing (Table 2.2, point 3).

Reflective Activity

To prepare yourself for the Written Exercise, consider how you would respond to the following scenarios by stating:

1. what you would do
2. when you would it
3. by what means.

Scenario 1: A parent makes a complaint that all her child does is play and is not learning how to read and write.
Scenario 2: A stranger walks across the outdoor play area to access the church yard that is adjacent to your setting.
Scenario 3: A colleague reports that another member of staff is walking around supervising groups of children while drinking a hot drink.

Group Exercise

The Group Exercise presents you with the opportunity to celebrate, share and discuss something that you have done to bring about change in your setting, network or service. This activity gives you the opportunity to demonstrate to your assessor how you effectively utilize your communication and interpersonal skills whilst interacting with other EYPS candidates.

Reflective Activity

Group Exercise

For this exercise, you will join three or four other candidates. You will be observed by two assessors. You will be informed in advance that you should be prepared to tell the other candidates about something you have done to bring about change in a setting. You will have four minutes for this. You should not use visual aids but should give the assessors a list of bullet points on a single side of A4 summarizing the main points you will cover. Keep a copy for yourself. The assessors will place a letter (A, B, C, D) on each candidate's seat: these will specify the running order. To assist time-keeping, Candidate D should advise Candidate A when four minutes have elapsed; Candidate A should do the same for Candidate B, Candidate B for

Candidate C, and Candidate C for Candidate D. In the event that you or another candidate exceeds the four minutes by more than 30 seconds, your assessor will intervene to stop the presentation. Once you have all completed this task, you have the remaining 14 minutes to discuss the presentations and draw some conclusions. The assessors will signal the start of the discussion, but you and the other candidates should ensure that you finish on time.

CWDC *Candidate Handbook* (2008a: 7)

During this exercise, you will need to conduct a four-minute presentation that you have prepared in advance. In your presentation, you will need to demonstrate a good working knowledge of national and local policies, procedures and frameworks and the EYFS 2008, and effective ways of leading colleagues through a period of change, irrelevant of how small the change is. Remember that your assessor will be making a judgement against the three generic skills illustrated in Table 2.2, p. 27 and that you may wish to consider including in your presentation:

1. The reasons for implementing the change and the time frame involved (Table 2.2, point 1).
2. Which national or local frameworks, policy or guidance that you researched to inform the change.
3. The range of colleagues and professionals that you consulted with to support you with the change (Table 2.2, point 1).
4. The influence that these changes had on your setting policies, practices and procedures (Table 2.2, point 1).
5. The way that you recognized and developed the potential of others during the change (Table 2.2, point 2).
6. The way that you proposed clear strategies for improvement as a change agent (Table 2.2, point 3).
7. The way that you listened to others' concerns about the change and how you made an informed response (Table 2.2, point 3).
8. How you supported your colleagues in a sensitive manner (Table 2.2, point 3).

I have listed eight points above for you to consider; that equates to speaking for half a minute (30 seconds) on each point, four minutes in total. The timing for each of the presentations in your group is crucial. You each get four minutes to make a presentation, and the remaining 14 minutes will be spent discussing each other's presentations and drawing up a list of commonalities to conclude the exercise. How you keep track of the time most effectively needs to be agreed at the start of the presentation. Throughout this exercise, you will need to be vigilant of your own and others' body language, for example maintain regular eye contact, be aware of facial expressions, which need to be positive and animated so that the other candidates feel that their views are valued, and avoid clenched fists! You also need to be aware of including everyone in the 14-minute discussion following the presentations – sometimes you may need to step back from the discussion and allow one of the other candidates to present their viewpoint or perception before articulating your own. Inviting a quieter member of the group into the conversation demonstrates an ability to include others. Being over-assertive in the discussion may demonstrate a dominating, authoritative leadership style.

To summarize, communicate confidently and clearly take ownership of your presentation, use the 'I' word, avoid saying 'we' when you talk about practice and events, listen and respond to other candidates' presentations in a sensitive and constructive manner, use good body language, value and respect other candidates' viewpoints, include everyone in the discussion and contribute to the overall conclusions (Table 2.2, point 3).

Interview with the Actor

Your training provider cannot promise Brad Pitt or Angelina Jolie but, in my experience, the actors that have been employed to perform this activity have assumed the role of an early years practitioner superbly.

 Reflective Activity

Interview with the actor

In this exercise, you will conduct an interview with an actor who is briefed to perform as a member of staff, a parent/carer or a peer professional. Before the interview starts, you will be given a briefing document. You will have 10 minutes to read it and prepare for the interview. You will be able to arrange the room as you wish. The actor will remain outside the room until, at the end of the 10 minutes of preparation time, you invite him or her into the room. You then have 15 minutes to conduct the interview. Your assessor will observe the interview, at the end of which you should leave the room.

CWDC *Candidate Handbook* (2008a: 9)

Table 9.3   *Reflections from EYPS candidates on the Gateway Review of Skills*

Interview with the Actor

'I found the role play challenging, but I enjoyed it more that I thought I would'

'The personal interview was interesting and not daunting as I expected, it was far more relaxed than I thought it would be'

'I was worried about time keeping and concluded the interview too quickly'

'I feel the role play was the weakest point, however in reality I would know the person and wouldn't be as timid back in my setting'

To prepare for your Interview with the Actor you will only be given 10 minutes to read your brief – after this, you will need to prepare yourself and arrange the room to your liking. Once the role play begins, you will assume the role of an EYP holding an interview with a member of staff, a parent/carer or another professional and be observed by your assessor. This activity potentially allows you to demonstrate your interpersonal leadership skills to your assessor who will be making a judgement against the three generic skills illustrated in Table 2.2. You will need to listen sensitively to the actor who will be in the role of a member of staff, a parent/carer or another professional, and conduct the interview in a way that is professional and concludes amicably.

At the start of the role play, welcome the actor (in the role of a member of staff, a parent/carer or another professional) into the room in the way that you normally would in your setting, network or service and make them feel at ease. Aim to identify any issues clearly and explicitly, which may be of concern either to you or the actor (in the role of a member of staff, a parent/carer or another professional).

While in your role of an EYP, you may wish to consider ways to:

✓ remain non-judgemental
✓ challenge stereotypical views and attitudes
✓ listen to and acknowledge personal feelings
✓ respond in a supportive manner
✓ manage personal feelings and use 'Emotional Intelligence'
✓ express your viewpoints professionally
✓ offer strategies for change.

The Interview with the Actor lasts for 15 minutes, so once again you will have to be very vigilant with your time-keeping and the pace at which you conduct the interview. In the eventuality of you running over the time specified, your assessor will stop the interview.

Table 9.4   *Examples of Gateway Review feedback*

Strengths in Leadership, Decision Making and Communication

Personal interview:
- You articulate your answers well and it shows that you are confident in your relationships with other colleagues and leadership.
- You showed how you liaised well with external agencies.
- You are developing your knowledge of the standards and have understanding of how to relate the standards to your practice and the written tasks.

Role play with actor:
- You showed very good listening skills and the ability to focus on the issue of X's concerns.
- You identified X's strengths and then used these to develop her confidence.
- Although X was reluctant to change her practice, you showed leadership qualities in finding ways to help develop her confidence.
- You communicated and conducted the interview professionally.

Written task activity:
- You sought out further information from other staff when needed to avoid making snap decisions (particularly in Tasks 1 and 2).
- Your writing was clear and legible.
- You took the opportunity to allow staff to develop their understanding of policies and procedures.
- You demonstrated the ability to be decisive yet were aware of the wider issues.
- Your response showed a high level of concern for others.

Group exercise:
- Your change example showed that you can identify key areas for development.
- You showed the ability to lead others through change with support and training.
- You showed respect for others and genuine interest in their presentations, through your comments and questions.
- You are able to reflect on changes made with a view to giving continuous support.

Development Points

Personal interview:
- Continue to explore the EYFS research, journals and the internet.
- Speak to your mentor and Local Authority team about training for the Common Assessment Framework (CAF).
- Continue to liaise with your mentor.

Role play with actor:
- In discussion, you did not always allow X to consider what you were saying, so aim to allow for more natural pauses in conversations.
- You frequently use 'OK' and could consider developing alternative phrases to use to show your empathy.

Written task activity:
- You might consider consulting the SENCO in Task X.
- You might have considered looking in more detail at learning through play in Task X.
- You could have phoned the parent immediately in Task X.

Group exercise:
- When giving a presentation, try to give the audience an overview at the start of your presentation rather than 'jumping straight in'.
- Try to organize your thoughts more clearly when giving presentations.
- Try speaking a little slower to allow the audience time to assimilate what you say.

Feedback from the Gateway Review of Skills

Point for Reflection

Written Reflection

Before you leave the venue, you will be asked to spend up to 20 minutes reflecting on your experience of the four exercises. You will be given a set of questions to help you do so. Your assessor will take account of these reflections when they prepare your feedback.

CWDC *Candidate Handbook* (2008a: 7)

The Gateway Review assessors are trained not to make any evaluative comments to you about the way that you have performed during or after any of the Gateway Review exercises.

Once all of your assessments have been completed, your training provider will collate the findings from your Gateway Review assessors and arrange to have them written up and sent to you. The content of the report will be based on the evidence directly derived from each of the four activities that you engaged in. The report will give you an indication of your strengths and areas for development related to each of the three generic skills assessed in the Gateway Review process (Table 2.2). This feedback will not contribute to your final EYPS assessment. In the eventuality that the evidence from your Gateway Review shows that you are not working at the right level or that you have a significant number of areas for development, then your training provider may advise you to defer undertaking the final stages of your assessment process or advise you to transfer to a different pathway. If this is the case, then you will not have to undergo the Gateway Review again.

You should discuss your feedback with your mentor or tutor who will be able to support you with the next stage of your assessment process. Table 9.4 provides an example of the type of feedback that you may receive from your training provider.

Key Points

Allow time to:
- ✓ Prepare yourself for the Gateway Review of Skills.
- ✓ Identify and analyse the EYPS standards.
- ✓ Map your knowledge, skills and understanding against the EYPS standards.
- ✓ Identify your strengths and development needs against the EYPS standards.
- ✓ Identify research, literature, statutory and non-statutory frameworks and training to support your Gateway Review Personal Interview.
- ✓ Prepare and rehearse your Gateway Review group presentation.
- ✓ Become aware of the way that you portray your interpersonal skills and body language in preparation for the role-play activity and the group presentation.
- ✓ Pin down the issue in the written exercises, and respond efficiently and effectively.
- ✓ Use the 'I' word in your assessments.
- ✓ Discuss the outcomes of your 'Gateway Review' with the mentor and use the feedback to support the final stages of assessment, the Written Tasks and the Setting Visit.

Further Reading

Children's Workforce Development Council (CWDC) (2008a) *Candidate Handbook: A Guide to the Gateway Review and Assessment Process*. London: CWDC.

Children's Workforce Development Council (CWDC) (2008b) *Guidance to the Standards for the Award of Early Years Professional Status*. London: CWDC.

Goleman, D., Boyatzis, R. and McKee, A. (2002) *Primal Leadership: Realizing the Power of Emotional Intelligence*. Harvard: Harvard Business School Press.

Rodd, J. (2006) *Leadership in Early Childhood*, 3rd edition. Maidenhead: Open University Press. (See especially Chapters 4, 5 and 7)

Useful Websites

Children's Workforce Development Council (CWDC) – www.cwdcouncil.org.ukeyps futures

Department for Children, Schools and Families (DCSF) (2008) *Building Brighter Futures: Next Steps for the Children's Workforce*. Available at: publications.everychild matters.gov.uk – reference 00292–2008.

Every Child Matters (and the Common Core of Skills and Knowledge) – www.everychild matters.gov.uk

CHAPTER 10

BEYOND THE GATEWAY

This chapter will explore the ways in which those seeking to gain EYPS can demonstrate their knowledge, skills and understanding of the 39 EYPS standards while preparing for the final stage of their assessment, the Written Tasks. This chapter reviews the requirements for each of the tasks and considers the nature of identifying documentary evidence to support your final assessment, the Setting Visit. This chapter will make links with Chapter 2, with reference to the final stage of the EYPS validation process which is the same for each of the four pathways. Links will be made to the theory in relation to the 39 EYPS standards discussed in Chapters 3 to 8. This chapter will provide the opportunity for reflective thinking in relation to identifying and recording the ways that the reader leads, models and supports their colleagues to continually improve their practice, establish and maintain positive relationships with children and develop their abilities to communicate and work in partnership with families, carers and other professionals.

The Written Tasks Assessment Process

As with the Gateway Review, you will undergo the same assessment process for the second phase of your assessments – the Written Tasks and the Setting Visit – which

Table 10.1   *EYPS written tasks*

Task 1: Lead and support other practitioners in implementing aspects of the EYFS for babies (0–20 months) – 1500 to 2000 words.
Task 2: Lead and support other practitioners in implementing aspects of the EYFS for toddlers (16–36 months) – 1500 to 2000 words.
Task 3: Lead and support other practitioners in implementing aspects of the EYFS for young children (30–60 months) – 1500 to 2000 words.
Task 4: An account of your personal practice with a child or children (of any age between birth and 60 months) – 1500 to 2000 words.
Task 5: Brief accounts of three situations or events – approximately 500 to 750 words for each situation.

Adapted from CWDC *Candidate Handbook* (2008a)

---

is the same for all candidates irrespective of which EYPS pathway is being followed. Your Written Tasks will comprise a series of reflective accounts of aspects of your work, and '… the process is concluded when an assessor visits the setting in which you are working or, if you are not based in a particular setting, a setting of your choosing. The evidence from your written tasks and the setting visit will demonstrate how you have met the Standards for EYPS. The written tasks will provide some evidence for all the 39 Standards, but the setting visit will corroborate and supplement the evidence of the tasks' (CWDC, 2008b: 5).

Your training provider will invite you to attend training to support you in writing up your Written Tasks. This training will help you to clarify your understanding of the Written Tasks, examine the depth of reflection required, the way that they need to be cross-referenced and the contribution that they make to showing how you meet the EYPS standards. Table 10.1 illustrates the range of Written Tasks that you will need to complete and the format in which they need to be presented. When you do your Written Tasks, remember to use the 'I' pronoun rather than 'we' when you are describing a situation or event. This is the same advice as given in the previous chapter for the Gateway Review of Skills activities. Remember that your assessor is interested in your contribution and not the contribution of your colleagues or your team.

For each of the Written Tasks, there are minimum and maximum numbers of words recommended (see Table 10.1). These have been set as a guideline (CWDC, 2008b) and your assessor will not count the exact number of words that you write. In summary, your Written Tasks are designed to allow you to demonstrate your personal practice, your leadership and support, and your knowledge and understanding of the early years sector against all of the EYPS standards.

Your training provider will provide you with templates for you to write up the Written Tasks. In these, you will need to describe, analyse and reflect on the activities and events that you decide to present, using the format specified by CWDC for each of the tasks. You have the opportunity to support your Written Tasks '… by a limited amount of documentary evidence associated with the activities' (CWDC, 2008b: 24). Any documentary evidence that you submit will be scrutinized by your assessor during your

Setting Visit. You must make sure that the ones you present are pertinent to your own practice and leadership of others.

The Nature of the Written Tasks

The tasks are designed in such a way as to allow you to record your competencies against the EYPS standards. You will need to demonstrate how the two elements of a) personal practice and b) leadership and support are demonstrated within each group of standards and not within each individual EYPS standard. To remind you, the groups of EYPS standards are:

✓ Knowledge and understanding (covered in Chapters 3 to 8).
✓ Effective practice (covered in Chapters 4 to 6).
✓ Relationships with children (covered in Chapter 7).
✓ Communicating and working in partnership with families and carers (covered in Chapter 7).
✓ Team work and collaboration (covered in Chapter 8).

Essentially, you must provide sufficient evidence of working with the three age groups (babies, toddlers and young children) across the standards; however, the extent and currency of the evidence will of course vary amongst the three age groups depending on your current and previous job roles.

You will need to reflect on and record 'real life' examples of your working practice. Hypothetical situations or events are not acceptable, nor can you describe something that you are planning to do or aiming to achieve in the future. The Written Tasks should evidence your experiences within the last three years. However, this being said, you '... may draw on evidence from the recent past. Any tasks based on previous work or experience should normally have taken place within the past three years. This time period acknowledges the possibility that, in your recent career, you may have worked with babies, toddlers and young children consecutively rather than concurrently. It also enables you to refer to occasional or seasonal activities' (CWDC, 2008b: 13–14).

The Task Assessment Grid

You will need to provide evidence for all of the EYPS standards across the five completed tasks. This does not mean that each individual task has to include reference to every one of the 39 EYPS standards. By the time you have completed all five of your Written Tasks, you must have made reference to every one of the EYPS standards. CWDC (2008b) have designed a Candidate Task Assessment Grid (see p. 166) to 'enable you to make explicit how you are meeting the Standards through your written tasks. Some Standards will be more easily met through one task than through another and the Task Grid provides a means by which you can keep track of which tasks provide evidence for each Standard. Any one of your written tasks will demonstrate more than one Standard, but you should avoid the temptation to use a single written task to try to demonstrate the majority of or all the Standards' (CWDC, 2008b: 13).

An example of a portion of a grid completed by a candidate for EYPS S1 using ticks

Std	1	2	3	4	5a	5b	5c	Assessor's evaluative comments	X? √
S1	√			√					

Source: CWDC (2008b: 13)

To help both you and your assessor to track the extent of your claims for each of the Written Tasks, you can either put a tick against each standard that you feel can be verified by your assessor (see the example above), or consider annotating the personal practice and/or leadership and support elements of the EYPS standards (see example below). To annotate your personal practice and/or leadership and support, you may wish to consider replacing the ticks with the letter 'P' to annotate Personal Practice and/or the letters 'L/S' to annotate Leadership and Support. This method of recording is not a CWDC mandatory requirement but may be helpful to you and your assessor.

An example of a portion of a grid completed by a candidate for EYPS S1 using 'P' to annotate Personal Practice and/or the letters 'L/S' to annotate Leadership and Support

Std	1	2	3	4	5a	5b	5c	Assessor's evaluative comments	X? √
S1	P			P+L/s					

Source: CWDC (2008b: 25)

Whichever way you decide to record your claims, I urge you to complete the Task Assessment Grid as you write up your tasks. It is very important for you to use the task evidence record as it allows you to record which standards you have covered and which ones you need to include. You will be asked to submit your Task Assessment Grid to your training provider alongside the Written Tasks by a set deadline. Your training provider will use this to check to see that you have claimed all the standards. If you fail to claim one or more of the standards, your work will be returned to you to rectify this and it may jeopardize the timing of your Setting Visit.

Written Tasks 1, 2 and 3

Tasks 1, 2 and 3 all follow the common format set by CWDC (2008b) (see Table 10.2) which you will use to record and evaluate your experiences of leading, promoting, implementing and monitoring the EYFS in your setting, network or service. These three tasks require you to report on activities that demonstrate how you led and supported your colleagues to implement the EYFS (DCSF, 2008b) with each of babies, toddlers and young children. You should outline and evaluate your experiences of leading, promoting, implementing and monitoring the EYFS in your own setting, network or service. Your accounts should be recorded on the template that your training provider provides. The word count for each of these tasks should be between 1500 to 2000 words. The type of activity that you write about can apply to either working with an individual colleague or with a wider group of colleagues.

Written Activity

Identify an example of a time that you have led and supported other practitioners to implement aspects of the EYFS within the past three years.

Task	Activity	EYPS Standards
Task 1: Babies (0–20 months)		
Task 2: Toddlers (16–36 months)		
Task 3: Young children (30–60 months)		

You cannot combine Tasks 1, 2 and 3 – they need to be individual reflections of activities that you have led at the level required to meet the EYPS standards. These

Table 10.2   *Format of Written Tasks 1, 2 and 3*

Lead and support other practitioners in implementing aspects of the EYFS for:

Task 1 – babies (0–20 months)
Task 2 – toddlers (16–36 months)
Task 3 – young children (30–60 months)

You will need to report on these activities within the following format:

- the nature of the activity
- the age range, in months, of the children directly or indirectly affected
- what you planned to do and why
- what happened when you carried out the work
- your assessment of the effectiveness of the activity
- your personal learning.

Adapted from CWDC *Candidate Handbook* (2008a)

three tasks will demonstrate key evidence of your experience of working with babies, toddlers and young children – as well as giving a description of the activity, you must also demonstrate how that activity was underpinned by your knowledge and understanding of effective practice in the EYFS (DCSF, 2008b) and working in partnership with families and carers, discussed in Chapters 4 to 7.

The format for the Written Tasks 1–3 is described in Table 10.2

You will need to set the scene by stating the nature of the activity that you are going to write about, including the children's ages, and recording the reason why you planned to do the activity. When you start to write up the section about what happened when you carried out the work, aim to structure your response and consider the following:

1   What knowledge and understanding am I showing in this activity? (EYPS standards 1–6)
2   What effective practice am I demonstrating in this activity? (EYPS standards 7–24).
3   What relationship with children am I including in this activity? (EYPS standards 25–28)
4   In what ways am I going to record the ways that I communicated and worked in partnership with families and carers? (EYPS standards 29–32)
5   How can I show the ways in which I led on team work and collaboration in this activity? (EYPS standards 33–36)
6   What professional development did I identify to support this activity (EYPS standards 37–39)

Don't forget to evaluate the effectiveness of the activity and write about your personal; learning. I always encourage my candidates to state this under the following two sub-headings:

- Personal learning about my own practice
- personal learning about my leadership and support of others.

Written Task 4

This CWDC task requires you to write a reflective account of your own personal practice with a baby, toddler or a young child or children (aged from 0 to 60 months). You can write about the way you led an adult-initiated or a child-initiated activity, or a combination of both. The format for Task 4 is illustrated below.

Table 10.3   *Format of Written Task 4*

An account of your personal practice with a child or children (of any age between birth and 60 months) – you will need to report on the activity within the following format:
<ul><li>the nature of the activities</li><li>the age range, in months, of the child or children involved</li><li>what they planned to do with the child/children, and why</li><li>what happened when they carried out the activity or activities</li><li>their assessment of the effectiveness of the activities</li><li>their personal learning.</li></ul>

Adapted from CWDC *Candidate Handbook* (2008a)

The format for the CWDC Task 4 activity refers to 'planning': if you decide to write about child-initiated activity, 'planning' may well refer to the way you made an informed decision to react spontaneously to the context of the child-initiated activity. Alternatively, you may wish to consider writing about the planning that resulted as a consequence of the activity. EYPS S10 asks you to show how you 'Use close, informed observation and other strategies to monitor children's activity, development and progress systematically and carefully, and use this information to inform, plan and improve practice and provision' (CWDC, 2008b). EYPS S11 asks you to 'plan and provide safe and appropriate child-led and adult-initiated experiences, activities and play opportunities in indoor, outdoor and in out-of-setting contexts, which enable children to develop and learn'(CWDC, 2008b). Refer to Chapter 4 to review the High/Scope 'plan, do and review approach' to planning, or the Te Whāriki, 'well being–belonging–contribution–communication–exploration' approach and the Leuven EXE 'well-being and involvement' model.

Written Activity

1. Identify an example an adult-initiated or child-initiated activity, or a combination of both, in your own personal practice with a child or children (of any age between birth and 60 months) in the past three years.
2. Select one of the activities to write about for EYPS Task 4.

EYPS Task 4	Activity	EYPS Standards
Babies (0–20 months)		
Toddlers (16–36 months)		
Young children (30–60 months)		

Whilst reflecting on your personal practice, consider making reference to the *Practice Guidance for the EYFS* (DCSF, 2008a: 7) which supports the notion that the role of the practitioner is crucial in:

- observing and reflecting on children's spontaneous play
- supporting and extending specific areas of children's learning
- extending and developing children's language and communication in their play.

Written Task 5

This task comprises three reflective reports on situations or events that you have encountered and that demonstrate your wider professional role. These three reflective reports can provide additional evidence to strengthen your claims against the EYPS standards, and also help you to fill in the gaps by providing evidence for EYPS standards that you have found it difficult to cover in the other tasks. As mentioned previously in this chapter, I always stress the importance of completing the Task Grid Assessment to my EYPS candidates as they progress – that way, by the time that they come to write up the final three reflective accounts for Task 5, they will know which EYPS standards need to be to covered. The CWDC (2008b) format that you will need to follow when writing up the Written Task is illustrated in Table 10.4.

Table 10.4   *Format of Written Task 5*

Brief accounts of three situations or events with either babies, toddlers or young children – you will need to report on the situations or events within the following format:

- a brief description of the situation or event
- your analysis of the situation
- your personal learning.

Adapted from CWDC *Candidate Handbook* (2008a)

Whatever activities or events that you decide to write up, they need to '... relate to routine encounters and do not have to relate to dramatic or extraordinary events. They may refer to challenging situations, but assessors are more interested in your work on routine professional issues rather than your experience in handling crises or dramatic situations' (CWDC, 2008b: 12).

Written Activity

EYPS Task 5:

1. Reflect on activities or events that demonstrate the ways in which your personal practice and your leadership and support have involved children, parents and carers, staff or other professionals, either inside or outside the setting in the past three years.
2. After reviewing your Task Assessment Grid to identify any gaps in standards, select three activities to write up Assessment for EYPS Task 5. These reflective reports can be from any of the age ranges.

EYPS Task 5	Activity	EYPS Standards
Babies (0–20 months)	What happened? Why did it happen? How were you involved?	
Toddlers (16–36 months)	What happened? Why did it happen? How were you involved?	
Young children (30–60 months)	What happened? Why did it happen? How were you involved?	

Prior to your Setting Visit, your assessor will be sent the complete set of your Written Tasks and any supporting documents so that they can begin to authenticate your claims against the standards and prepare themselves for your Setting Visit assessment. Your assessor can best be described using the metaphor of a detective trying to record evidence. This may sound like a tenuous link, but rest assured your assessor will be very skilful at seeking out the evidence to substantiate your claims against the EYPS standards.

Any reference that you make to your colleagues, babies, toddlers and young children or other adults must be anonymous. Just like the evidence you present when the inspector calls for an Ofsted inspection, the Written Tasks will only provide a snapshot of you, your practice and your leadership and support of others. In your Written Tasks, aim to accentuate your strengths, paint an accurate pen picture about yourself, your personal practice, your leadership and support and your achievements. In the final part of the Written Task template, you must reflect on what impact your actions have made and write an effective evaluation. In the section entitled 'Your Personal Learning' (on the Written Task template), I always advise my candidates to insert the headings: (a) Personal Practice and (b) Leadership and Support. This allows them to demonstrate their learning under the heading that the assessors will be interested in.

By the time that you have completed all five tasks, each relating to different aspects of your personal practice and your leadership and support, you will have covered all 39 EYPS standards. The final chapter (Chapter 11) will expand on the purpose and nature of the Written Tasks and allow you to prepare yourself for the final stage of your EYPS assessment journey, the Setting Visit.

Key Points

✓ The assessment process is the same for all candidates irrespective of which EYPS pathway they are following.

✓ The Written Tasks comprise a series of reflective accounts of aspects of your personal practice and leadership and support.

✓ The evidence from your Written Tasks is used to form the basis of your Setting Visit assessment.

✓ You must provide sufficient evidence of working with the three age groups (babies, toddlers and young children) across the standards in the Written Tasks.

✓ The extent and currency of the evidence in your Written Tasks will vary amongst the three age groups depending on your current and previous job roles.

✓ Hypothetical situations or events are not acceptable in the Written Tasks, nor can you describe something that you are planning to do or aiming to achieve in the future.

✓ Any Written Tasks must be based on previous work or experience that has normally taken place within the past three years.

✓ You cannot combine Tasks 1, 2 and 3 – they need to be individual reflections of activities that you have led at the level required to meet the EYPS standards.
✓ Once all five tasks, each relating to different aspects of your personal practice and your leadership and support, have been completed, you will have covered all 39 EYPS standards.

Further Reading

Children's Workforce Development Council (CWDC) (2008a) *Candidate Handbook: A Guide to the Gateway Review and Assessment Process.* London: CWDC.
Children's Workforce Development Council (CWDC) (2008b) *Guidance to the Standards for the Award of Early Years Professional Status.* London: CWDC.
Rodd, J. (2006) *Leadership in Early Childhood,* 3rd edition. Maidenhead: Open University Press.

Useful Websites

Children's Workforce Development Council – www.cwdc.org.uk
Department for Children, Schools and Families (DCSF) (2008) *Building Brighter Futures: Next Steps for the Children's Workforce.* Available at publications.everychildmatters. gov.uk – reference 00292-2008
Muijs, D., Aubrey, C., Harris, A. and Briggs, M. (2004) 'How do they manage? A review of the research in Early Childhood', *Journal of Early Childhood Research,* 2: 157. Available at ecr.sagepub.com/cgi/content/abstract/2/2/157

CHAPTER 11

THE FINAL STAGES OF THE EYPS VALIDATION PROCESS – THE SETTING VISIT

This final chapter will pull together the various strands presented in preceding chapters to support your preparation for the final EYPS validation process, the Setting Visit assessment. It will draw your attention to the documentary evidence that you will need to gather prior to the visit and the range of documents that you will need to submit to your training provider prior to the event. The chapter goes on to discuss ways that you can prepare yourself, your colleagues and your nominated witnesses for a positive outcome. The final part of the chapter will guide you through the stages of the visit and the ways in which your assessor will search for verification that you have met the EYPS national standards. The chapter will be further strengthened by the addition of links to previous chapters.

Preparing Yourself for the Final Assessment

Just like preparing to go on holiday, there are a number of things that you will need to do to ensure that the arrangements for your Setting Visit go to plan. To prepare yourself for the final stage of your EYPS journey, you must make time available to identify and collate a range of documentary evidence that you will organize in a file of 'supporting documentary evidence'. This is used by your assessor during your Setting Visit to verify your competencies against the standards. Your documentary evidence file must include examples of things that you have been involved in or contributed to, for example documentary evidence to support the case study of the EYP candidate who worked collaboratively with an Early Years Specialist Teacher in Chapter 6 may include a copy of the Early Years Specialist Teacher's notes of the visit.

Most fundamentally, before your Setting Visit can take place, your training provider will ask you to submit your Written Task and Setting Visit documentation by the set deadline.

Examples of the documents that you will be required to submit include:

- a set of Written Task response sheets for each of Tasks 1, 2, 3, 4 and 5
- a completed task grid, either ticked for each standard or annotated to show Personal Practice (P) and/or Leadership and Support (L/S)
- the list of documents included in the documentary evidence file
- a timetable of the Setting Visit
- an explanation about the tour of the setting
- a detailed Setting Visit form.

The CWDC *Candidate Handbook* (2008a) provides details about the range and type of documents that need to be submitted, however before you can complete the detailed CWDC Setting Visit form, you will need to confirm the following:

- the date of access to the setting with the owner or owner/manager
- that the setting will be operating normally on the date of the Setting Visit
- the availability of your three witnesses and the time of their interviews
- the timetable of the Setting Visit
- that a private area can be designated for the use of the assessor.

Your detailed CWDC Setting Visit form will set the scene for your assessor; on it, you will confirm the date, the venue and time of the visit and provide relevant contact details. It is of paramount importance to complete this accurately. You may be able to negotiate the date of your Setting Visit within reason of your assessor's availability, however it is a formal national assessment process and this may not always be possible.

The Setting Visit Timetable

You should check the current CWDC *Candidate Handbook* (2008a) regarding the timetable for the Setting Visit – the duration and specified order of the activities must be followed except for unavoidable circumstances, in which case you will have to inform your training provider. Two examples of Setting Visit timetables are presented below.

Setting Visit Timetable Example 1 (CWDC, 2008a: 13)

08.20 Arrival: meet candidate and setting manager, if appropriate
08.30 First interview with candidate on standards
08.50 Candidate's explanation of the organization of the file of supporting evidence
09.00 Scrutiny of file of supporting documentary evidence
10.15 Tour of the setting
11.00 Write up of tour notes on the Visit Response Sheet and reflection time
11.30 Witness interviews
12.30 Lunch
13.00 Reflection time, preparing for the second interview with the candidate
13.30 Second interview with candidate on standards
14.00 Visit concluded

Setting Visit Timetable Example 2 (CWDC, 2008a: 14)

10.20 Arrival: meet candidate and setting manager, if appropriate
10.30 First interview with candidate on standards
10.50 Candidate's explanation of the organization of the file of supporting evidence
11.00 Tour of the setting
11.45 Write up of tour notes on the Visit Response Sheet and reflection time
12.15 Lunch
12.45 Scrutiny of file of supporting documentary evidence
14.00 Witness interviews
15.00 Reflection time, preparing for the second interview with the candidate
15.30 Second interview with candidate on standards
16.00 Visit concluded

Accommodating Your Assessor

It is vitally important for you to arrange a designated area for your assessor to use during the duration of the Setting Visit. This area needs to be private and free from disruptions, as your assessor will be undertaking:

An EYP candidate discussing the documentary evidence wtih her assessor

- a scrutiny of your documentary evidence
- two personal interviews with you
- three interviews with your nominated witnesses
- a final informed judgement about your performance against the EYPS standards based on the evidence gathered during the day.

Another reason for ensuring that the area is private is to avoid any possibility that a well-meaning colleague or a child might strike up a conversation which potentially may distract the assessor. CWDC (2008a: 13) acknowledge that 'in some settings, this may be problematic; for example, if the one available room doubles up as a staff room and office and is in constant use. However, it is in your interests to ensure that suitable arrangements are made for the day of the visit. If you do have any problems, discuss them with your provider. If you are a childminder, your assessor will appreciate the circumstances under which you may be working'. Your assessor will need to spend 5 hours and 40 minutes at the setting of your choosing and there is no restriction on when the visit should start or finish, but the 5 hours and 40 minutes should normally be consecutive and the start time should be in agreement with yourself and your assessor.

Preparing 'Documentary Evidence'

Your training provider will ask you to compile a portfolio of documentary evidence, within a small A4 ring binder, which will be shown to your assessor during the Setting

An EYP candidate preparing his documentary evidence

Visit assessment. You are not required to submit your supporting file of documentary evidence with your Setting Visit documentation as you will have 10 minutes to present and discuss the documents in your file with your assessor during the Setting Visit – please see the Setting Visit Timetable Examples 1 and 2 on page 174. The way that you organize your file is at your own discretion, however when you submit your Written Tasks to your training provider, you will need to include a list of the supporting documentary evidence and signpost the rationale for the choice of each document. In doing this, let your assessor know how the documents demonstrate your personal practice and/or your leadership and support – don't leave your assessor guessing.

You may also wish to consider referencing the standards that the document pertains to. The documents that you choose to include in your documentary evidence file must be relevant and recent (within the past three years) and they may or may not be related to your Written Tasks unless you so choose. In my experience of assessing candidates, it is the depth not the breadth of your documentary evidence file that counts. Your assessor will only have a limited amount of time to scrutinize the documents presented and too many documents can be overwhelming and distract the assessor from the key documents. You may include up to five Witness Statements in your documentary evidence. These statements should provide evidence about your performance against the EYPS standards and corroborate an element of your personal practice and/or your leadership and support, for example one of your colleagues may write a supporting statement about a time that you led and supported a change in the setting, network or service. Avoid including any Witness Statements that focus on your personal attributes, for example 'x is really nice with the children'. This type of statement does not provide concrete evidence about your performance against the standards, and it will be viewed by your assessor as an assertion, because it does not give any evidence about your practice other than the fact that you are nice.

Examples of documentary evidence that you may wish to include could be 'assessment records; plans; minutes of meetings; reports; case studies; observation notes; notes from parents and carers; memos from staff and other professionals; audits of resources' (CWDC, 2008a: 15). Reports from other professionals confirming the actions that you have taken personally as part of a consultation or multi-agency activity may also be considered. These would act as a primary source of evidence, for example for S6: 'The contribution that other professionals within the setting and beyond can make to children's physical and emotional well-being, development and learning' (CWDC, 2008a: 20), you may consider including a copy of a report written by a SENCO confirming the way that you have supported your colleagues' understanding of specific behaviour management strategies for an individual child.

Identifying Witnesses

Before you submit a detailed Setting Visit form, you will need to identify three witnesses who you feel will corroborate your claims about your personal practice and/or your leadership and support whilst being interviewed by your assessor. Their names, job roles and the reasons why they have been selected will need to be recorded on your Setting Visit form. Examples of witnesses that you may wish to consider include:

- your setting manager
- a practitioner who reports to you
- a colleague who you may have trained or mentored
- another professional from the Local Authority advisory service
- another setting manager that you have supported
- a Childminding Network coordinator.

It is always a good idea to brief your witnesses before the Setting Visit. Try to make it clear that neither they nor the staff in the setting nor indeed the setting itself are being assessed. Your assessor's questions will primarily focus on the standards and will require your witnesses to give tangible examples rather than express assertions. As discussed previously, your assessor is not trying to find out if you are a lovely person or if you can be really friendly to parents – they are seeking tangible examples of your personal practice and/or your leadership and support. I would advise you to discuss the purpose of the interviews with your witnesses, to show them a copy of the EYPS standards and inform them about the requirements of the EYPS award. Let them know that the assessor may ask them to give examples, like 'how does X promote health and safety in the setting?' Let them know that the assessor may probe for further evidence, by asking 'how does X encourage the team to follow these strategies?' Your witnesses should also be informed that during their interviews, the assessor will record the responses to the questions asked as near as word-verbatim as possible, and this sometimes means that they will have to speak slowly and specifically.

CWDC (2008a: 16) acknowledge that in some settings, 'it will not be uncommon for one family member to act as line manager to another, particularly in private settings, and it would be inequitable to deny such candidates the opportunity to call a line manager as witness. If this applies to you, you should declare this kind of connection in writing before the start of the setting visit'.

The arrangements for witnesses interviews will vary depending on the availability of your witnesses – the examples of the Setting Visit timetable, discussed previously in this chapter, suggest that an hour will be spent interviewing your witnesses, one at a time. However, it is permissible to interview parents in pairs as it is universally accepted that parents may often feel intimidated by such a formal arrangement. Two parents will only count as one witness. In the eventuality of one of your witnesses being unavailable on the day, either due to a personal or professional reason, then it is accepted that it would be unreasonable to expect them to travel to the setting and in such circumstances the assessor may conduct a telephone interview. 'It is your responsibility to arrange for telephone interviews to take place at an appropriate time during the setting visit' (CWDC, 2008a: 16). You will also have to make sure that the assessor has access to a telephone and that your witness telephone numbers are at hand.

The Setting Visit

The Setting Visit is the final destination of your journey to gain the EYPS status but remember that it is not just the destination that your assessor will be interested in. It is more the way that your personal practice and/or your leadership and support have developed over the journey. As mentioned previously in this chapter, before the visit can take place, your assessor should have received the Setting Visit documentation listed in the CWDC *Candidate Handbook* (2008a). The purpose of the Setting Visit is to provide you with an opportunity to provide both verbal and written evidence of your personal practice and/or your leadership and support in the setting, in relation to the EYPS standards. I find the whole process of the Written Tasks, the candidate and witness interviews, the scrutiny of the documentary evidence and the tour of the setting amazing – it allows the assessor to triangulate your evidence and corroborate your claims against the standards. *Flaubert's Parrot* (Barnes, 1985) which I urge you to read demonstrates the lengths that a researcher has to go to corroborate any evidence presented.

'The purpose of the setting visit is twofold:

- first, to provide you with an opportunity to provide both oral and documentary evidence of your work in the setting, relative to the Standards; and
- second, to enable your assessor to complement the evidence of your written tasks through a scrutiny of your documentation, a tour of your setting and through talking to you and your nominated witnesses' (CWDC, 2008a: 12).

The Extent of the Visit

Your Setting Visit will include everything that is illustrated in the examples of the Setting Visit timetables discussed previously in this chapter, for example your assessor will conduct:

- an initial interview with you relating to the EYPS standards and your Written Tasks
- a scrutiny of your supporting file of documentary evidence
- a tour of your setting
- three interviews with your nominated witnesses who are familiar with your personal practice and/or your leadership and support (either in the setting or by telephone)
- a final interview with you concerning specific standards
- two periods, each of 30 minutes, for private reflection.

The First Interview with Your Assessor

Before your visit, your assessor will have decided on the standards that they will use to influence any questions that they may ask you. Any questions asked will be phrased skilfully by the assessor in order to illicit a response from you that will complement what you have written about in your Written Tasks, thus giving you the opportunity to demonstrate more fully your personal, professional practice and/or your leadership and support. As with the standards interview that you undertook as part of your Gateway Review of Skills (see Chapter 9), your assessor will be making a word-verbatim record of your responses in the interview, so please appreciate that you will need to speak slowly and that your assessor may not be maintaining normal eye contact.

Your assessor may ask you to describe your role within and relationship with the setting. Although some of the questions may be pre-determined by the assessor in advance of the visit, you will be asked supplementary ones and your assessor may very well probe until they get the responses they are looking for. Remember that the questions will be aimed at determining your personal knowledge and experience relative to certain EYPS standards, so listen very carefully to the questions phrased. There are some techniques that you may wish to adopt to support you, for example:

- ✓ Prepare yourself and focus on the positive changes that you have made.
- ✓ Review your responses to the written tasks.
- ✓ Know your personal qualities.
- ✓ Know the early years sector and the statutory and non-statutory frameworks.
- ✓ Know the EYPS standards.
- ✓ Avoid using the pronouns 'we' or 'they'. Use the pronoun 'I'.
- ✓ Aim to give examples of your own personal practice and/or your leadership and support.
- ✓ Define your contribution to any activity discussed.
- ✓ Always ask your assessor for clarification if the question is unclear.
- ✓ Avoid talking in general terms, for example 'I always make sure that the parents are informed', rather than describing a specific example about informing the parents about an activity or event.
- ✓ When the assessor asks for an example, have two or three at the ready.
- ✓ Avoid um and er when hesitating.

Remember that the interviews are time-bound and your assessor will conclude the interview within the specified time frame.

Scrutiny of the Documentary Evidence

The format for the scrutiny of the documentary evidence was discussed previously in this chapter. You will have submitted a list of the documents (that your assessor will be in possession of) indicating clearly the number of documents and the reasons for their selection. You will need to use this list at the start of the process to explain the layout of your file to your assessor and how it 'relates to the Standards and to other evidence (from your written tasks and your nominated witnesses)' (CWDC, 2008a: 14). CWDC have allocated 10 minutes for you to do this in consultation with your assessor. It is important that you present a well-organized file to support your assessor's ability to make judgements against the documents you have provided. I once assessed a candidate who presented me with a document folder stuffed with documents saying that they had not had the time to organize it – unfortunately neither had I and important documents may well have been overlooked. If for any reason you cannot include 'all the necessary supporting documentary evidence in your file, possibly because it is in frequent demand by other staff or it is confidential and is in a secure location, it is your responsibility to make sure the assessor can consult this evidence with minimum inconvenience both to your assessor and to your colleagues' (CWDC, 2008a: 15).

Tour of the Setting

The tour of the setting is definitely not like an Ofsted inspection – your assessor is only interested in what impact you have made! Prior to the Setting Visit, you will have submitted a written summary of the main areas to be seen on the tour to your assessor. In your summary, you will have made reference to the EYPS standards to highlight the contribution that you have made to the indoor and outdoor environment. Your assessor will make notes on this document as you show them around the setting. Although your assessor will see you within the context of the day-to-day operations of the setting, they are not there to observe you in practice – the aim of the tour is for you to explain to your assessor the contribution that you have made to the setting. However, 'during the tour, it may be diplomatic not to disclose some information to your assessor in the hearing of colleagues, parents, carers or children' (CWDC, 2008a: 15).

Obviously, the structure of the tour will vary depending on the type of setting in which you are based, for example the tour will be very different whether you are a childminder in your own home environment, someone working in a large day nursery or in a pre-school run in a church or village hall. As you guide your assessor around the setting, you will explain how each area (indoors and outdoors) or room has been set up and why, talk about any special features and explain how practice varies for individual babies, toddlers and/or young children.

There are some strategies that you may wish to adopt to support you with the tour, for example:

- review the summary of the tour of the setting that you submitted to your training provider with your documentary evidence and think carefully about what you want your assessor to see
- take control of the tour – before you start the tour, brief your assessor about what they are going to see
- use the summary of the tour to provide you with starting points for the commentary that you will give during the tour
- avoid using the pronouns 'we' or 'they', aim to say 'I' organized
- show your assessor all parts of the setting, indoors and outdoors
- introduce your assessor briefly to any members of staff that you meet on the tour

An EYP candidate on a tour of the outdoor setting

- explain your contribution to each area and say why it has been organized the way that it has
- highlight any special areas that you have made a significant contribution to
- explain how you influence the environment, resources and practice for individual babies, toddlers and young children
- direct the assessor's attention to the way that you have organized or influenced child observations and record keeping
- highlight your contribution to parent notice boards and displays
- draw attention to any health and safety signage or risk assessment documents that you have implemented
- show how you influence inclusive practice in the setting.

While showing your assessor around the setting, in my experience, it is almost inevitable that a child will come running up to you bursting with something to say. The way that you respond to the child is a wonderful opportunity for you to demonstrate your ability to communicate sensitively (EYPS S26) or listen to what they have to say (EYPS S27). Despite the fact that your assessor is not there to observe you in practice, they may very well pick up on your relationships with the babies, toddlers and the young children and indeed with your colleagues or parents and carers. At the end of the tour of your setting, your assessor will have 30 minutes of reflection time to write up the evidence that they have gleaned from the tour and to make their judgements against the standards (see the Setting Visit Timetable).

By this stage of your Setting Visit assessment, your assessor will be starting to build a rich picture of your personal practice and your leadership and support against each group of the EYPS standards. Your assessor will use this information to inform the final two stages of the Setting Visit assessment, the witness interviews and your final candidate interview.

Witness Interviews

The selection process for your choice of witnesses was discussed previously in this chapter. To assist your assessor, the detailed Setting Visit form that you submitted prior to your training provider provided the:

- name of each witness
- the reasons for selecting them
- their position
- the order in which each witness will be interviewed
- the timing for each witness interview (one hour to be divided between all three – this does not have to be equal).

Earlier on in the chapter, it was suggested that you may wish to brief your witnesses about the nature and purpose of the interviews. Remember that the assessor is not assessing them but will be assessing you! The EYPS assessors are trained to be very skilful in their approach and they will put your witnesses at ease. Assessors follow the same procedures nationally and they will always check the name and position of your witness. Their questions will be standards-related, however assessors understand that some of your witnesses may be new to the profession or indeed have very little knowledge of the sector. If this is the case, your assessor will ask the questions in a manner that takes this into account.

Points for Reflection

Examples of questions that the assessor might ask witnesses:

- ✓ 'How do you know ...?'
- ✓ 'Can you tell me how ... leads and supports the delivery of the EYFS?' (S1)
- ✓ 'How does ... influence policies and procedures in the setting?' (S35)
- ✓ 'Tell me how ... communicates with children?' (S25, S26, S27and S15)
- ✓ 'Does ... support you to use and develop ICT in the setting?' (S37)
- ✓ 'What is ... relationship with parents?' (S30)
- ✓ 'What are ... qualities as a team player?' (S33)
- ✓ 'How does ... contribute to child observations and planning?' (S10 and S11)

The Final Interview

The final part of your journey to gain EYPS status culminates in an interview with your assessor. Prior to the start of your interview, your assessor will have had 30 minutes of reflection time, as detailed on the Setting Visit timetable discussed earlier in this chapter. This is to provide your assessor with the opportunity to triangulate all the evidence that they have ascertained from your interviews, your witnesses interviews, your documents and the tour of the setting, to determine whether or not they need to raise any further lines of questioning with you. Just like your first interview and the standards review interview at your Gateway Review of Skills, your assessor will be recording what you say word-verbatim and you should speak slowly and succinctly. Your assessor may use the opportunity to shed light on anything that has cropped up during the day or to tie up any loose ends. Be prepared to:

- clarify anything that the assessor has seen or been told during the day
- explain your understanding of national and local frameworks, for example the EYFS (2008) (DCSF, 2008b) or the DCSF *Children's Plan* (2007b)
- explain how you keep yourself and your colleagues up to date with national and local legislation and policy
- provide additional information about the way that you work in partnership
- discuss the way that you promote relationships with parents.

Make certain that you use this opportunity to tell your assessor about anything that you feel you need to, as this is your last opportunity!

Unfortunately, your assessor will not be able to give you any indication of the outcome of your assessment at this stage. Your assessor still has some work to do before your assessment is internally moderated by your training provider and then sent off to the CWDC national external moderation before you will receive your result. Rest assured that your assessor will have worked hard to verify your claims against the standards.

  Key Points

✓ The Written Task and the Setting Visit documentation must be submitted by the set deadline.
✓ Check the current CWDC *Candidate Handbook* (2008a) regarding the timetable for the Setting Visit.
✓ Arrange a designated area for your assessor to use during the duration of the Setting Visit.

✓ The documents that you choose to include in your documentary evidence file must be relevant and recent (within the past three years) and they may or may not be related to your Written Tasks unless you so choose.

✓ Identify three witnesses who you feel will corroborate your claims about your personal practice and/or your leadership and support and brief them about the process.

✓ The purpose of the Setting Visit is to provide your assessor with an opportunity to seek both verbal and written evidence of your personal practice and/or your leadership and support against all of the EYPS standards.

✓ Adopt strategies and techniques to prepare yourself for your interviews and the tour of the setting.

✓ Any Written Tasks must be based on previous work or experience that has normally taken place within the past three years.

✓ There are rising expectations from the government that the early years will be reformed and that our provision will become one of the best in the world.

✓ The EYPS assessment process is not completed until the final outcome is announced following the CWDC national moderation.

Further Reading

Cooke, G. and Lawton, K. (2008) *For Love or Money: Pay, Progression and Professionalism in the Early Years Workforce*. London: Institute for Public Policy Research.

Children's Workforce Development Council (CWDC) (2008a) *Candidate Handbook: A Guide to the Gateway Review and Assessment Process*. London: CWDC.

Children's Workforce Development Council (CWDC) (2008b) *Guidance to the Standards for the Award of Early Years Professional Status*. London: CWDC.

Goleman, D., Boyatzis, R. and McKee, A. (2002) *Primal Leadership: Realizing the Power of Emotional Intelligence*. Harvard: Harvard Business School Press.

Useful Websites

Children's Workforce Development Council – www.cwdcouncil.org.ukeypsfutures

Department for Children, Schools and Families (DCSF) (2008) *Building Brighter Futures: Next Steps for the Children's Workforce*. Available at publications.everychild matters.gov.uk – reference 00292-2008

Every Child Matters: and the Common Core of Skills and Knowledge – www.everychild matters.gov.uk

CONCLUDING COMMENTARY

The concluding commentary will examine the main issues raised with the introduction of the new EYP and possible answers offered for further debate by the reader. The concluding thoughts will be around the transformational role of the practitioner as an early years change agent and the imperative need to identify and establish a collective vision that supports children's learning and development, a culture of collaborative team working underpinned by shared values, a shared commitment to parents and carers and a personal commitment to continued professional development.

The EYPS validation process will have taken you on a very long reflective leadership journey. Each candidate's journey will have been different, as you all had different starting points. You all lead in different ways and in different roles. Along the way you will have reflected upon the knowledge and understanding and the skills and behaviours that are expected of you in your role. Gaining the EYP status is the start of things to come and once you have achieved it you will become a key player in the government's Early Years transformation agenda. Jane Harwood the chief executive of CWDC reported that 'The first EYPs are already making a difference to the lives of children. Their enthusiasm, commitment and skill is impressive and I look forward to seeing their impact spread across the early years world'. CWDC (2008b: 04).

Becoming an EYP is not all about being someone who will control the entire fate of the early years sector per se. EYPs are here and now – you may never lead a multinational early years organization but you will lead best practice, project teams, multiprofessional teams and colleagues in your early years setting, in order to bring about better outcomes for children and their families.

Your leadership skills will continue to grow and develop and you will never stop learning about leadership. I advocate that all early years leaders should read *Who Moved My Cheese?* by Spenser Johnson (1999). The cheese should be viewed as a metaphor for what many of us in the early years sector are striving to achieve. It is a short and clever story of four mice going through a period of change. The behaviours of the mice may be very familiar to you – two of the mice are stuck in their old ways of living, while the other two imaginatively seek a new way to survive.

It cannot be denied that there is still much work to be done in the early years sector and we need the support of the government and the Local Authority to achieve this. There may be times when leadership feels like being in a maze. At times, we are able to orientate ourselves through the pathways and, at other times, we can be led down blind alleys and have to start the process all over again. Despite this, you do not have to wait until you achieve great heights to show that you are a capable leader – leaders exist at all levels in the early years sector. There are still issues around pay, progression and recognition. EYPS is a newly claimed status and as leaders you must play a role in tackling these issues.

Challenges for the Future Role of the EYP

In this book, we have discussed the fact that the future of the early years looks very promising. We have looked at the importance of the early years British government policy and its current high profile. It is now essential that EYPs are taken seriously. The way that we have traditionally motivated ourselves in the early years sector is to be congratulated – many of us have worked long hours, and we have often responded to both national and local initiatives, policies and guidance innovatively and with resilience. 'There is a renewed emphasis on pre-school provision and EC programmes which is both encouraging and entirely necessary, if some of the fundamental disadvantages in society are to be successfully addressed' (Muijs et al., 2004).

Your journey recognized that working in partnership with parents and carers can often be rewarding and, at other times, the level of responsibility can be overwhelming. You will be very aware that there is a real mixed bag of provision in the sector. Despite the commitment and support of the government, Local Authorities and the early years workforce itself, there still exists a postcode lottery as to where babies, toddlers and young children will receive the best outcomes. As an EYP, you will help to overturn this over a period of time. You may have looked at the government work-force reforms to offer accessible, affordable childcare, which are tied in to getting people back to work and training and reducing poverty and inequalities, you will need to keep yourself up to date with strategies to continue this.

Your colleagues will need supporting with the government's new integrated qualification framework. While it offers your colleagues the opportunity to transfer their skills and work across the early years sector, many who qualified previously will find that their qualifications no longer hold the currency deemed necessary to drive the reforms. Your enthusiasm and commitment to continuing professional development will support your colleagues to make the necessary transitions. In so doing, they will need your support to reflect on new ways of working, examine the ways that work well, what can be improved and ways that they can bring about better outcomes for children and families.

Having taken on a leadership role, you may very likely get bogged down with administration, inspection regimes and audits, leaving you more often than not with very little time to do what is so very close to your hearts, that is, play with the children! Despite all this, it is a very exciting time to be leading practice in the early years and there are rising expectations from the government that the early years will be reformed and that our provision will become one of the best in the world. As a newly qualified EYP, you must be supported in your role – the government has pledged to support your continuing professional development and you may well be invited to join your local authority EYP network. Your aspirations as a newly qualified EYP need to be recognized and made to become a reality, in order to prevent them from becoming a government initiative that only makes minimal impact.

In summary, the one thing that we can all be certain of is that early years provision will change and that we collectively need to be there to influence those changes for the generations of babies, toddlers and young children to come and for the colleagues that we work with. This book has invited you to review a wide range of early years research literature, local and national frameworks and policies and tools to aid your skills as a reflective practitioner and your understanding about what it means to be an EYP. However, as the Government's agenda to transform the early years sector continues to be revised and implemented you will need to keep yourself up to date with any new developments and interpret them within the parameters of your own pedagogical values and beliefs. As your leadership journey continues, consider Covey's (2004: 95) *Second Habit of Highly Effective People'*, 'Always begin with the end in mind'. My book is not only there to support your journey to become an EYP, it is also there as guide to support you in the years that follow.

GLOSSARY

The following terms and abbreviations are used throughout this book:

Adult-Child Ratio   A ratio of the qualified practitioners to children in a child care setting.

Attachment   A psychological bond between adult and child.

Appraisal   A two way discussion between a practitioner and their line manager focusing particularly on personal development, EYFS targets, training needs and resources needed.

Best Practices   A term used to denote the ways of delivering services that have been found through research or experience as the "best" ways to achieve desired outcomes

Candidate   The term used to describe the person who is undertaking the EYPS training.

Child Protection   A term used to explain everything that needs to be done to protect a child or young person from significant harm and neglect.

The Common Assessment Framework (CAF)   A nationally standardized approach to conducting an assessment of the needs of a child or young person and deciding how those needs should be met.

Child Development   The process by which a child acquires skills in the areas of social, emotional, intellectual, speech and language, and physical development, including fine and gross motor skills. Developmental stages refer to the expected, sequential order of acquiring skills that children typically go through. For example, most children crawl before they walk. or use their fingers to feed themselves before they use utensils.

Child Observations   Observed measurement of a child's cognitive, language, knowledge and psychomotor skills in order to evaluate development in comparison to children of the same chronological age and plan appropriately for the next steps in learning.

Developmental Milestone   A term used to describe a memorable accomplishment on the part of a baby or young child; for example, rolling over, sitting up without support, crawling, pointing to get an adult's attention, or walking.

Developmentally Appropriate   A way of describing practices, that are adapted to match the age, characteristics and developmental progress of a specific age group of children.

Developmentally Appropriate Practice   A concept of EYFS practice that reflects knowledge of child development and an understanding of the unique personality, learning style and family background of each child.

Continuous Professional Development (CPD)   In the early years field, the term refers to opportunities for child care providers to get ongoing training to increase their preparation and skill to care and educate children. These include in service training, nationally accredited early years programmes and Higher Education Foundation Degree or degree programmes.

Children's Workforce Development Council (CWDC)   CWDC is a national organization established in 2005 to support the implementation of Every Child Matters, a new approach to the well-being of children and young people from birth to age 19. CWDC works in the interest of over half a million people in the children's workforce across England.

EYAT   An Early Years Advisory Teacher employed by the Local Authority to support early years settings

Early Years Foundation Stage (EYFS)   The statutory framework for the education and welfare of children from birth to the 31 August following their fifth birthday.

Early Support   Early Support is the central government mechanism for achieving better coordinated family-focused services for very young disabled children and their families.

Early years providers   Includes those who are registered on the Early Years Register to provide for children from birth to the 31 August following their fifth birthday.

Early years provision   The provision for the learning, development and care of children from birth to the 31 August following their fifth birthday.

Early years settings   Childminders, day nurseries, playgroups and children's centres not deemed to be schools who provide for children from birth to the 31 August following their fifth birthday.

Early Childhood Environmental Rating Scale (ECERS)   A research-based assessment instrument to ascertain the quality of early care and education programs. The scale is designed for classrooms of children ages $2\frac{1}{2}$-5 years. It is used to assess general classroom environment as well as programmatic and interpersonal features that directly affect children and adults in the early childhood setting.

EYP   Early Years Professional

EYPS   Early Years Professional Status

Families   The term 'families' is used to cover parents and carers.

Free Flow Play   An unpressured time for children to choose their own play activities, with a minimum of adult direction. Practitioners may observe, intervene, or join the play, as needed. Free flow play may be indoors or outdoors.

GLF   Graduate Leader Fund

Gross Motor Skills   A child's development of large muscle movement and control.

Inclusion   The principle of enabling all children, regardless of their diverse abilities, to participate actively in the early years setting.

ITERS-Infant Toddler Environment Rating Scale   A 35-item instrument designed to evaluate the quality of a child care setting for infants and toddlers. The scale is divided into 7 areas: furnishings and displays for children; personal care routines; listening and talking; learning activities; interaction; program structure; and adult needs.

Learning Disability   An impairment in a specific mental process which affects young children's (0-5 yrs) learning.

Mentors   Experienced early years care and education or professionals who have personal and direct interest in the development and/or education of young children (0-5 yrs.).

Foundation Stage practitioner   A person who works directly with children aged 0-5 years in a Foundation Stage setting.

National Quality Improvement Network (NQIN)   Working with the Department for Children, Schools and Families, the National Children's Bureau has set up a national peer support network: the National Quality Improvement Network

Ofsted   The Office for Standards in Education, Children's Services and Skills – came into being on 1 April 2007. It brings together the wide experience of four formerly separate inspectorates. It will inspect and regulate care for children and young people.

Personal Development Plan   A list of what an individual needs to do and how they will do it. It will identify new skills to be developed and the training necessary for this to happen.

Portfolio   A folder containing evidence of your own practice and leadership and support of others.

Private, Voluntary and Independent (PVI)   Private, voluntary and independent (PVI) providers of childcare for the under fives, these include, full daycare, sessional datcare for children under 5, and childminders caring for children under 5

Safeguarding and promoting the welfare of children   This is protecting children from abuse and neglect and helping children and young people get the most from life.

Sessional day care   A child care arrangement where children attend on a regular normally they operated for three to four hours per day.

Special Educational Needs   A baby, toddler or young child under the age of 5 who requires a level of care and education to meet their specific need.

Special Educational needs Co-ordinator (SENCO)   The role of the SENCO supports early identification and intervention for children with special educational needs. The SENCO is responsible for maintaining a setting's recording and documentation process with respect to special educational needs, liaising and working with the parents, securing training for workers and liaising with outside agencies with respect to a child's SEN.

Setting   The early education or childcare place of work, this may include pre-schools, nurseries, Sure Start children's centre's and childminders

Safeguarding Board   An official public agency, responsible for receiving and investigating reports of suspected abuse or neglect of children and for ensuring that services are provided to children and families to prevent abuse and neglect.

Sure Start   A government programme which aims to deliver the best start in life for every child. It brings together early education, childcare, health and family support. Sure Start covers a wide range of programmes both universal and those targeted on particular local areas or disadvantaged groups within England.

The local Safeguarding Children Board   Is a team of senior people from different services in the Local Authority. The Board's job is to make sure all of the local services work together well to promote and safeguard children's and young people's welfare

Validation   A process through which candidates on the EYPS programme go through to meet the 39 specific standards to receive endorsement from CWDC.

EYPS STANDARDS

Those awarded Early Years Professional Status must demonstrate through their practice that they meet all of the following Standards.

Knowledge and Understanding

Those awarded Early Years Professional status must demonstrate through their practice that a secure knowledge and understanding of the following underpins their own practice and informs their leadership of others.

S01: The principles and content of the Early Years Foundation Stage and how to put them in to practice.

S02: The individual and diverse ways in which children develop and learn from birth to the end of the foundation stage and thereafter.

S03: How children's well-being, development, learning and behaviour can be affected by a range of influences and transitions from inside and outside the setting.

S04: The main provisions of the national and local statutory and non-statutory frameworks within which children's services work and their implications for early years settings.

S05: The current legal requirements, national policies and guidance on health and safety, safeguarding and promoting the well-being of children their implications for early years settings.

S06: The contribution that other professionals within the setting and beyond can make to children's physical and emotional well-being, development and learning.

Effective Practice

Those awarded Early Years Professional Status must demonstrate through their practice that they meet all the following Standards and that they can lead and support others to:

S07: Have high expectations of all children commitment to ensuring that they can achieve their full potential.

S08: Establish and sustain a safe, welcoming, purposeful, stimulating and encouraging environment where children feel confident and secure and are able to develop and learn.

S09: Provide balanced and flexible daily and weekly routines that meet children's needs and enable them to develop and learn.

S10: Use close, informed observation and other strategies to monitor children's activity, development and progress systematically and carefully, and use this information to inform, plan and improve practice and provision.

S11: Plan and provide safe and appropriate child-led and adult initiated experiences, activities and play opportunities in indoor, outdoor and in out-of-settings contexts, which enable children to develop and learn.

S12: Select, prepare and use a range of resources suitable for children's ages, interests and abilities, taking account of diversity and promoting equality and inclusion.

S13: Make effective personalised provision for the children they work with.

S14: Respond appropriately to children, informed by how children develop and learn and a clear understanding of possible next steps in their development and learning.

S15: Support the development of children's language and communication skills.

S16: Engage in sustained shared thinking with children.

S17: Promote positive behaviour, self-control and independence through using effective behaviour management strategies and developing children's social, emotional and behavioural skills.

S18: Promote children's rights, equality, inclusion and anti-discriminatory practrice in all aspects of their practice.

S19: Establish a safe environment and employ practices children's health, safety and physical, mental and emotional well-being.

S20: Recognise when child is in danger or at risk of harm and know how to act to protect them.

S21: Assess, record and report on progress in chidren's development and learning and use this as a basis for differentiating provision.

S22: Give constructive and sensitive feedback to help children understand what they have achieved and think about what they need to do next and, when appropriate, encourage children to think about, evaluate and improve on their own performance.

S23: Identify and support children whose progress, development or well-being is affected by changes or difficulties in their personal circumstances and know when to reger them to colleagues for specialist support.

S24: Be accountable for the delivery of high quality provision.

Relationships with children

Those awarded Early Years Professional Status must demonstrate through their practice that they meet all the following Standards and that they can lead and support others to:

S25: Establish fair, respectful, trusting, supportive and constructive relationships with children.

S26: Communicate sensitively and effectively with children from birth to the end of the foundation stage.

S27: Listen to children, pay attention to what they say and value and repect their views.

S28: Demonstrate the positive values, attitudes and behaviour they expect from children.

Communicating and working in partnership with family and others

Those awarded Early Years Professional Status must demonstrate through their practice that they meet all the following Standards and that they can lead and support others to:

S29: Recognise and respect the influential and enduring contribution that families and parents/carers can make to childrens development, well-being and learning.

S30: Establish fair, respectful, trusting and constructive relationships with families and parents/carers, and communicate sensitively and effectively with them.

S31: Work in partnership with families and parents/carers, at home and in the setting, to nurture children, to help them develop and to improve outcomes for them.

S32: provide formal and informal opportunities through which information about children's well-being, development and learning can be shared between the setting and families and parents/carers.

Teamwork and collaboration

Those awarded Early Years Professional Status must demonstrate that they:

S33: Establish and sustain a culture of collaborative and cooperative working between colleagues.

S34: Ensure that colleagues working with them understand their role and are involved appropriately in helping children to meet planned objectives.

S35: Influence and shape the policies and practices of the setting and share in collective responsibility for their implementation.

S36: Contribute to the work of a multi-professional team and, where appropriate, coordinate and implement agreed.

Professional development

Those awarded Early Years Professional Status must demonstrate through their practice that they meet all the following Standards and that they can lead and support others to:

S37: Develop and use skills in literacy, numeracy and information and communication technology to support their work with children and wider professional activities.

S38: Reflect on and evaluate the impact of practice, modifying approaches where necessary, and take responsibility for identifying and meeting their professional development needs.

S39: Take a creative and constructively critical approach towards innovation, and adapt practice if benefits and improvements are identified.

REFERENCES

Adair, J. (1983) *Effective Leadership*. London: Pan.

Arnold, C. (2001) 'Persistence pays off: working with hard to reach parents', in M. Whalley and the Pen Green team, *Involving Parents in their Children's Learning*. London: Paul Chapman Publishing.

Aubrey, C. (2007) *Leading and Managing in the Early Years*. London: Sage.

Barnes, J. (1985) *Flaubert's Parrot*. London: Picador.

Barton, D. and Hamilton, M. (1998) *Local Illiteracies: Reading and Writing in One Community*. London: Routledge.

Belbin, M. (1981) *Management Teams: Why they Succeed or Fail*. London: Routledge.

Belenky, M., Clinchy, B., Goldberger, N. and Tarule, J. (1986) *Women's Ways of Knowing: The Development of Self, Voice, and Mind*. New York: Basic Books.

Bennis, W. (1989) *On Becoming a Leader*. Reading, MA: Addison-Wesley.

Blanchard, K. (2007) *Leading at a Higher Level*. Harlow: Pearson Education.

Blanchard, K., Zigarmi, P. and Zigarmi, D. (2004) *Leadership from the One-minute Manager*. London: HarperCollins.

Bolam, R. (1999) 'Educational administration, leadership and management: towards a research agenda', in T. Bush, L. Bell, R. Bolam, R. Glatter and P. Ribbins (eds), *Educational Management Re-defining Theory, Policy and Practice*. London: Paul Chapman Publishing.

Booth, T., Ainscow, M. and Kingston, D. (2006) *Index for Inclusion: Developing Play, Learning and Participation in Early Years and Childcare*. Bristol: Centre for Studies on Inclusive Education.

Brock, A. and Rankin, C. (2008) *Communication Language and Literacy from Birth to Five*. London: Sage.

Bruce, T. (2006) *Early Childhood: A Guide for Students*. London: Sage.

Bruce, T. and Spratt, J. (2008) *Essentials of Literacy*. London: Sage.

Brunel University (2008) www.brunel.ac.uk/about/hongrads/2005/sugar (accessed 22 September 2008).

Bruner, J. (1983) *Child's Talk: Learning to Use Language*. New York: W.W. Norton.

Bruner, J. (1996) *The Culture of Education*. Cambridge, MA: Harvard Unversity Press.

Bush, T. and Middlewood, D. (1997) *Managing People in Education*. London: Paul Chapman Publishing.

Bush, T. and Middlewood, D. (2005) *Leading and Managing People in Education*. London: Sage.

Carr, M. and May, H. (2000) 'Te Whariki: curriculum voices', in H. Penn (ed.), *Early Childhood Services: Theory, Policy and Practice*. Oxford: Open University Press.

Children's Workforce Development Council (CWDC) (2006) *A Head Start for All*. London: CWDC.

Children's Workforce Development Council (CWDC) (2007a) *The Lead Professional: A Manager's Guide*. London: CWDC.

Children's Workforce Development Council (CWDC) (2007b) *Common Assessment Framework: Managers' and Practitioners' Guides*. Available at www.everychildmatters.gov.uk (accessed 22 September 2008).Children's Workforce Development Council 2007.

Children's Workforce Development Council (CWDC) (2008a) *Candidate Handbook: A Guide to the Gateway Review and Assessment Process*. London: CWDC.

Children's Workforce Development Council (CWDC) (2008b) *Guidance to the Standards for the Award of Early Years Professional Status*. London: CWDC.

Claxton, G. (2002) *Building Learning Power*. Bristol: Henleaze House.

Covey, S. (2004) *The Seven Habits of Highly Effective People*. London: Simon and Schuster.

Cox, E. (1996) *Leading Women: Tactics for Making the Difference*. Sydney: Random House.

Cubillo, L. (1999) 'Gender and leadership in the NPQH: an opportunity lost?', *Journal of In-service Education*, 25(3): 381–91.

Curren, D. (1998) *Working with Parents: A Guide to Successful Parent Groups*. Minneapolis: American Guidance Service.

David, T., Gouch, K., Powell, S. and Abbott, L. (2007) 'Being safe and protected'. DfES Research Report No. 444: Birth to Three Matters – A Review of the Literature. Nottingham: Queen's.

Department for Children, Schools and Families (DCSF) (2007a) *Letters and Sounds: Principles and Practice of High Quality Phonics*. Available at www.standards.dfes.gov.uk/primary/publications/literacy/letters_sounds/ (accessed 22 September 2008).

Department for Children, Schools and Families (DCSF) (2007b) *Children's Plan – Building Brighter Futures*. Norwich: HMSO.

Department for Children, Schools and Families (DCSF) (2008a) *Practice Guidance for the Early Years Foundation Stage*. Nottingham: DCSF.

Department for Children, Schools and Families (DCSF) (2008b) *Statutory Framework for the Early Years Foundation Stage*. Nottingham: DCSF.

Department for Children, Schools and Families (DCSF) (2008c) *Section 2: The Learning and Development Requirements, Communication, Language and Literacy. The Statutory Framework for the Foundation Stage*. Nottingham: DCSF.

Department for Children, Schools and Families (DCSF) (2008d) *Section 2: Assessment Arrangements. The Statutory Framework for the Foundation Stage*. Nottingham: DCSF.

Department for Children, Schools and Families (DCSF) (2008e) *Early Support Programme*, available at www.every childmatters.gov.uk.(accessed 22 September 2008).

Department for Education and Employment (DfEE) (2000) *Curriculum Guidance for the Foundation Stage*. London: Qualifications and Curriculum Authority.

Department for Education and Skills (2001) (DfES) *Special Educational Needs Code of Practice*. Nottingham: DfES Publications.

Department for Education and Skills (DfES) (2002) *Birth to Three Matters: A Framework to Support Children in their Earliest Years*. Norwich: DfES.

Department for Education and Skills (DfES) (2003a) *National Standards for Under-8s Day Care and Childminding*. London: DfES. (Revised 2005.)

Department for Education and Skills (DfES) (2003b) *Every Child Matters: Change for Children*. London: The Stationery Office.

Department for Education and Skills (DfES) (2004a) *Choice for Parents, the Best Start for Children: A Ten-year Strategy for Childcare*. Norwich: DfES.

Department for Education and Skills (DfES) (2004b) *Statutory Guidance on Making Arrangements to Safeguard and Promote the Welfare of Children under Section 11 of the Children Act 2004 – Every Child Matters: Change for Children*. Nottingham: DfES.

Department for Education and Skills (DfES) (2004c) *KIDSactive/SureStart – All of Us: Inclusion checklist for settings*. Nottingham: DfES.

Department for Education and Skills (DfES) (2004d) *Playing with Sounds: A Supplement to Progression in Phonics*. London: DfES.

Department for Education and Skills (DfES) (2004e) *Every Child Matters: Next Steps*. London: DfES.

Department for Education and Skills (DfES) (2005a) *Children's Workforce Strategy: A Strategy to Build a World-class Workforce for Children and Young People – Consultation Document* Nottingham: DfES.

Department for Education and Skills (DfES) (2005b) *Key Elements of Effective Practice (KEEP): Primary National Strategy*. Nottingham: DfES.

Department for Education and Skills (DfES) (2006a) *Children's Workforce Strategy: The Government's Response to the Consultation*. Nottingham: DfES.

Department for Education and Skills (DfES) (2006b) *Code of Practice on the Provision of Free Nursery Education Places*. Nottingham: DfES.

Department for Education and Skills (DfES) (2007) *The Early Years Foundation Stage – Effective Practice: Inclusive Practice*. London: HMSO.

Department for Work and Pensions (2005) Disability Discrimination Act. Available at www.dwp.gov.uk/aboutus/business.asp (accessed 22 September 2008).

Directorate for Education (2004) *Starting Strong Curricula and Pedagogies in Early Childhood Education and Care: Five Curriculum Outlines*. Stockholm: OECD.

Draper, L. and Duffy, B. (2001) 'Working with parents', in G. Pugh (ed.), *Contemporary Issues in the Early Years: Working Collaboratively for Children*. London: Paul Chapman Publishing.

Ebbeck, M. and Waniganayake, M. (2003) *Early Childhood Professionals: Learning Today and Tomorrow*. Sydney: MacLennan and Petty.

Eden, C. and Vangen, S. (1994) 'The language of collaboration.' Paper presented at the 2nd International Workshop on Multi-organisational Partnerships: Working Together across Organisational Boundaries, Glasgow, June.

Formosinho, J. (2003) 'Transformational leadership in early childhood centres.' Conference paper, Pen Green Centre, Corby.

Freedom in Education (2008) Available at www.freedom-in-education.co.uk/ (accessed 22 September 2008).

General Teaching Council for England (GTC) Nursing and Midwifery Council (NMC) and General Social Care Council (GSCC) www.gtce.org.uk/standards/professional/joint_ statement (accessed 1 February 2009).

Goleman, D. (1996) *Emotional Intelligence: Why it Can Matter More Than IQ*. London: Bloomsbury.

Goleman, D., Boyatzis, R. and McKee, A. (2002) *Primal Leadership: Realizing the Power of Emotional Intelligence*. Harvard: Harvard Business School Press.

Handy, C. (1976) *Understanding Organizations*, 3rd edn. London: Penguin.

Harms, T. (2004) *Early Childhood Environment Rating Scale (Ecers-R)*. Gloucestershire: Teachers College Press.

Harms, T., Cryer, D. and Clifford, R.M. (2002) *Infant/Toddler Environment Rating Scale*. Gloucestershire: Teachers College Press.

Harris, B. (2007) *Supporting the Emotional Work of School Leaders*. London: Paul Chapman Publishing.

Hatch, M.J. (2000) *Organization Theory*. Oxford: Oxford University Press.

Howes, C. and Hamilton, C.E. (1993) 'The changing experience of child care changes in teachers and in teacher–child relationships and children's social competence with peers', *Early Childhood Research Quarterly*, 8: 15–32.

Howes, C., Mattheson, C.C. and Hamilton, C. (1994) 'Maternal, teacher and child care history correlates to children's relationships with peers', *Child Development*, 65: 264–73.

Huczynski, A. and Buchanan, D. (1991) *Organizational Behaviour*. Hertfordshire: Prentice-Hall.

Humphries, E. and Sendon, B. (2000) 'Leadership and change: a dialogue of theory and practice', *Australian Journal of Early Childhood*, 25(1).

Johnson, S. (1999) *Who Moved My Cheese?* London: Vermillion.

Kennedy, C. (1998) *A Guide to the Management Gurus: Shortcuts to the Ideas of Leading Management Thinkers*. London: Century Business.

Laevers, F. (ed.) (1994) *Defining and Assessing Quality in Early Childhood Education*. Belgium: Laevers University Press.

Law, S. and Glover, D. (2000) *Educational Leadership and Learning Practice: Policy and Research*. Buckingham: Open University Press.

Leighton, A. (2007) *Allen Leighton on Leadership*. London: Random House Business Books.

Margaret Mcmillan – details available at www.spartacus.schoolnet.co.uk/Wmcmillan.htm (accessed 22 September 2008).

Marin, C. (2007) 'Empowering early years practitioners: a comment on the SiCs self-assessment instrument at network on early childhood education and care' summary record of the 2nd workshop – 'Beyond Regulation: Effective Quality Initiatives in ECEC'. Brussels: OECD.

McCall, C. and Lawler, H. (2000) *School Leadership: Leadership Examined*. London: The Stationery Office.

Montessori Society AMI – details available at: www.montessori-uk.org/calen.htm (accessed 22 September 2008).

Mooney, A. and Munton, A. (1997) *Research and Policy in Early Childhood Services: Time for a New Agenda*. London: Thomas Coram Research Unit, Institute of Education.

Moyles, J. (2006) *Effective Leadership and Management in the Early Years*. Maidenhead: Open University Press/McGraw-Hill Education.

Muijs, D., Aubrey, C., Harris, A. and Briggs, M. (2004) 'How do they manage? A review of the research in Early Childhood', *Journal of Early Childhood Research*, 2: 157. Available at ecr. sagepub.com/cgi/content/abstract/2/2/157

National Children's Bureau (NCB) (2008) *National Quality Improvement Network*. London: NCB.

National College for School Leadership. *Programme Leaders' Guide National Professional Qualification in Integrated Leadership*.

National Quality Improvement Network (NQIN) (2007) *Quality Improvement Principles*. London: National Children's Bureau.

National Quality Improvement Network (NQIN) (2008) *Companion Guide to the Quality Improvement Principles*. London: National Children's Bureau.

Neaum, S. and Tallek, J. (2002) *Good Practice in Implementing the Pre-school Curriculum*. Cheltenham: Nelson Thornes.

Nurse, A.D. (2007) *The New Early Years Professional*. Oxon: Routledge.

Nutbrown, C. (2006) *Key Concepts in Early Childhood Education and Care*. London: Sage.

Office for Standards in Education (Ofsted) (2007a) *Getting on Well: Enjoying Achieving and Contributing*. London: Ofsted.

Office for Standards in Education (Ofsted) (2007b) *Early Years: Firm Foundations*. London: Ofsted.

Office for Standards in Education (Ofsted) (2008) *Framework for the Registration of those on the Early Years and Childcare Register*. London: Ofsted.

Overall, L. (2007) *Supporting Children's Learning: A Guide for Teaching Assistants*. London: Sage.

Owen, J. (2005) *How to Lead*. Harlow: Pearson Education.

Papatheodorou, T. (2004) 'Assessing quality in the early years: early childhood environment rating scale – extension (ECERS-E) four curricula subscales'. Bristol: ESCalate Subject Centre web review, available at escalate.ac.uk/169 (accessed 31 October 2008).

Parker, C. (2002) 'Working with families on curriculum: developing a shared understanding of children's mark making', in C. Nutbrown (ed.), *Research Studies in Early Childhood Education*. Stoke-on-Trent: Trentham.

Peters, T. and Waterman, R. (1982) *In Search of Excellence*. New York: Harper and Row.

Potter, C.A. and Hodgeson, S. (2007) 'Language-enriched pre-school settings: a Sure Start training approach', in J. Schneider, M. Avis and P. Leighton (eds), *Supporting Children and Families: Lessons from Sure Start for Evidence-based Practice*. London: Jessica Kingsley.

Pugh, G. and Duffy, B. (2006) *Contemporary Issues in the Early Years,* 4th edn. London: Sage.

Oussoren R. (2001), *Write Dance: A Progressive Music and Movement Programme for the Development of Pre-Writing and Writing Skills*. London: Paul Chapman Publishing.

Reggio Children (2000) *The Hundred Languages of Children,* 3rd edn. Reggio Emilia: Reggio Children.

Rodd, J. (2006) *Leadership in Early Childhood*, 3rd edn. Maidenhead: Open University Press.

Rutter, M. (1995) 'Clinical implications of attachment concepts: retrospect and prospect', *Journal of Child Psychology and Psychiatry*, 36(4): 549-71.

Schein, E.H. (1992) *Organizational Culture and Leadership*. San Francisco: Jossey-Bass.

Siraj-Blatchford, I. and Manni, L. (2006) 'The Eleys Study'. Institute of Education, ectraspoce University of London. Available at www.gtce.org.uk/shared/contentlibs/126795/93128/120213/eleysstudy.pdf

Siraj-Blathford, I. Sylva, K., Muttock, S., Gildon, R. and Bell, D. (2002) 'Researching Effective Pedagogy in the Early Years', report no. 356. Institute of Education, University of Norwich: Department for Education and Skills.

Sylva, K., Siraj-Blatchford, K. and Taggart, B. (2003) *Assessing Quality in the Early Childhood Environment Rating Scale Extension (Ecers-E)*. Staffordshire: Trentham Books.

Sylva, K., Melhuish, E.C., Sammons, P., Siraj-Blatchford, I. and Taggart, B. (2004) *The Effective Provision of Pre-School Education (EPPE) Project: Final Report*. London: DfEE/Institute of Education, University of London.

Taylor, J. and Woods, M. (1998) *Early Childhood Studies: An Holistic Introduction*. London: Arnold.

Trevarthen, C. (1995) 'The child's need to learn a culture', *Children and Society*, 9(1): 5-19.

United Nations (1989) *Convention on the Rights of the Child*. New York: United Nations.

Whalley, M. (2003) 'The Pen Green Leadership Centre: Developing leadership learning and growing learning communities.' Paper presented at the 8th Early Childhood Convention, Palmerston North, 22–25 September.

Whalley, M. (2005) *National Professional Qualification in Integrated Centre Leadership: Roll Out Training Guidance*. Nottingham: National College for School Leadership.

Whalley, M. and the Pen Green Team (1997) *Involving Parents in their Children's Learning*. London: Paul Chapman Publishing.

Whalley, M.E., Allen, S. and Wilson, D. (2008) *Leading Practice in Early Years Settings*. Exeter: Learning Matters.

Whitehead, M. (1996) *The Development of Language and Literacy*. London: Paul Chapman Publishing.

Whitehead, M. (2002) *Developing Language and Literacy with Young Children*. London: Paul Chapman Publishing.

Yukl, G.A. (2002) *Leadership in Organizations*, 5th edn. Upper Saddle River, NJ: Prentice-Hall.

INDEX

Added to a page number 'f' denotes a figure and 't' denotes a table.